MITCHELL FAMILY

Best of
How to
Haunt Your
House

Volume II

Dozens of Spirited DIY Projects for Parties
and Halloween Displays

SCHIFFER
PUBLISHING

4880 Lower Valley Road • Atglen, PA 19310

ISBN: 978-0-7643-6199-9
Printed in India

Published by Schiffer Publishing, Ltd.
4880 Lower Valley Road
Atglen, PA 19310
Phone: (610) 593-1777; Fax: (610) 593-2002
E-mail: Info@schifferbooks.com
Web: www.schifferbooks.com

DEADICATION

We love our fear of the unknown. We like mysterious cold spots and things that make us jump. We smile at being caught off guard and laugh often when something makes our hair stand on end. We are at home with ghosts and spooks and creaky doors. It's Halloween again—*our favorite time of the year.* Time to embrace our fear of the dark and things that go bump in the night!

Neighbors will start to notice odd structures going up in our backyard in early August. Strange lights are often spotted in the late-night hours, and the occasional stray sounds of owls, hissing cats, and long, drawn-out cries of wolves will be heard echoing down the driveway. By October, a permanent thick, gray fog will hover over our house as a multitude of fog machines are set into place and tested. The jack-o'-lanterns will be lit and the skeletons hung. Endless yards of cobweb will be strung from every nook and cranny. The cauldron will be filled and candy will come out. The animated black crow will call out, *"It's time! It's Halloween time again!"*

Suspense will build as this new Hallows' Eve approaches. There will be many to peek through our fence for a preview. We know they will tell their children that the sign has been posted by the roadside, inviting all once again to take a tour of the Mitchell Cemetery. It is here that spirits move around fallen stones of old and rise up from mounds of fresh-dug graves of earth . . . visible to the sometimes-frightened eyes of passersby. Some won't make it past the open gate at the entrance. Others won't want to leave . . . amazed at all the glowing tombstones and ghosts that walk around to greet them. Costumed hands of the smallest visitors will hold tight to Mom and Dad and even tighter to plastic pails full of candy. It is our greatest joy to think that these brave souls will one day tell stories about the house on *Penton Street* . . .

This book offers a glimpse of what once was — a memory of a Halloween's past — and is dedicated to all those like us. We hope a chill runs up your spine and your hair stands on end, and more than once, you will glance over your shoulder at the unknown sounds in the night. Listen. Listen carefully for that childlike voice inside to say, *"It's Halloween time again . . . "*

The Mitchell Family

CONTENTS

Basic Tools & Materials
You Can Use for Most Projects

 hether you're a hardcore home haunter, a recrafter of store-bought items, or looking to create the most *spooktacular* party there ever was, there are a few handy tools to have on hand before you start.

1 Craft paints
Black and white craft paints are essential. Other colors such as red, brown, green, and yellow could also be used.

2 Gauze or cheesecloth
You'll find many uses for this versatile, lightweight material. It can be dyed, torn, painted, and wrapped.

3 Drywall compound
This is excellent for creating textures on all kinds of props and can be mixed with latex paint for a starting base color. Once dry, it can be painted further and made to resemble everything from marble to wood.

4 Woodburning or soldering tool
These tools are perfect for sculpting detail into Styrofoam. Different woodburning tips can achieve a variety of effects. The heated tool melts Styrofoam quickly, but the results can be everything from chiseled stone to lettering. Use in a well-ventilated area.

5 Craft brushes
A variety of craft brush sizes are always handy for applying final details to props.

6 Serrated knife
A serrated knife is useful for cutting Styrofoam. It creates a rough, uneven edge.

7 Craft glue
Water-soluble craft glue or Gorilla glue will work for most projects and can be used on Styrofoam.

8 Toothpicks
Toothpicks are like straight pins for the home-haunter. They are perfect for holding parts in place for a variety of projects in this book. Use the type that is pointed on both ends.

9 Hot-glue gun & glue sticks
The hot-glue gun is the best tool in the home-haunter's arsenal. Have several bags of glue sticks on hand to start with.

10 Heated wire cutter
Another tool for cutting and carving Styrofoam is the wire Styrofoam cutter. It creates smooth edges.

11 L brackets
Any woodbuilding projects that use the 1" x 2" wood will also use lots of L brackets to join the two pieces of wood together at the corners.

12 PVC pipe
Strong yet lightweight, PVC is used in making interior, bone structures, fence poles, and candle forms. Many sizes and thicknesses are available.

13 Duct tape
An all-around useful material in a variety of projects is duct tape. Use to shape a character's body or hold project pieces in place while you work.

14 Wood & wood screws
Excellent for building large prop structures or as interior skeletons of prop characters. Generally, 1" x 2" wood is used. Heavier wood can also be used for extra stability.

15 Styrofoam
Styrofoam is found in hardware stores and is used as insulation in houses. Styrofoam comes in a variety of thicknesses, from half inch to 2" thick. There are two types of Styrofoam; white foam has a larger cell structure and comes in sheets of the largest thickness. Blue *(or pink)* foam has a tighter composition and is less messy than white foam when cut but is available only in thinner sizes. Full sheet size is 4' by 8'. Styrofoam is great for creating large, lightweight walls or several tombstones per sheet.

16 Wiper motor, wall wart, or pacemaker; quick-connect power supply cord
If you want to animate your props, these are some basic components you will need. *See page 94 for more details on motor projects.*

17 Other useful items
Carbon paper, black and white spray paint, latex gloves, paver sand, zip ties, fabric dye, wire, wire cutters, PVC cutter, drill and drill bits, wax paper, Plexiglas, carpet glue, rope, pipe insulation, spray bottle, cardboard building form tube, polymer clay, polymer clay mold forms, jewelry charms, beads or buttons, Styrofoam prop skulls and bones, faux fur, cages of various sizes and shapes, large- and small-sized jars, plastic cauldron, pond misters, Christmas lights, chicken wire, clothes hanger, old clothes or curtains.

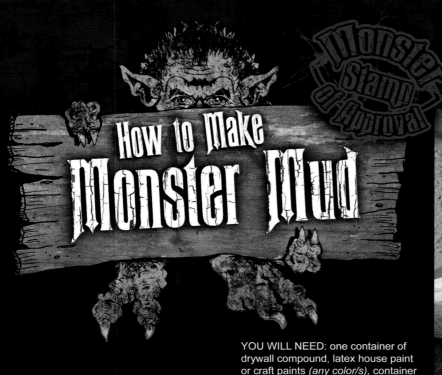

How to Make Monster Mud

YOU WILL NEED: one container of drywall compound, latex house paint or craft paints *(any color/s)*, container for mixing, spoon or drywall mixer attachment, and drill to mix large batches *(optional)*

Small-batch mixing

Monster Mud is a term first coined by Steve Hickman of Terror Syndicate Productions; however, the recipe and application have been used in the effects industry for some time. It is simple to make and can be applied to an unlimited list of craft projects that require some texture. It also works very well with Styrofoam. The Monster Mud creates a textured shell over the lightweight Styrofoam that can then be made to look like a variety of materials. Recycle some of that old paint sitting in the garage. It doesn't matter what colors you use or mix. It will be used as a base for other colors on the Styrofoam "stone." How much compound is needed depends on the project. Make a large batch in a bucket with a lid and you can store it for months. Mix roughly five parts drywall compounds to one part latex paint and mix. A drywall mixer attached to a drill works best to mix large batches. A spoon and bowl will work for small batches. Use latex gloves and protect clothing and surfaces. Monster Mud will stain.

Drywall compound

Latex paint mixed with drywall compound for sand-colored base

Mix any color of craft paints for base color

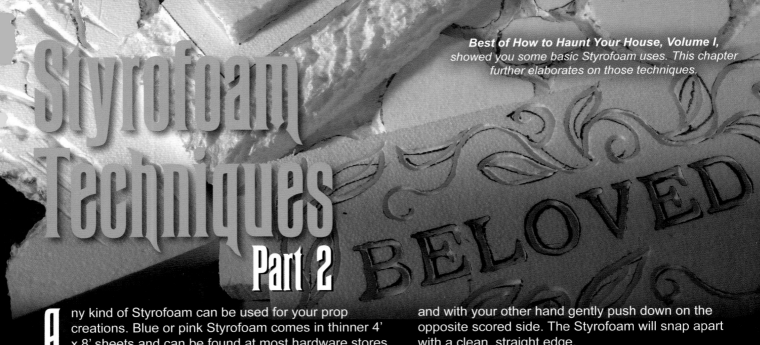

Styrofoam Techniques
Part 2

Best of How to Haunt Your House, Volume I, showed you some basic Styrofoam uses. This chapter further elaborates on those techniques.

Any kind of Styrofoam can be used for your prop creations. Blue or pink Styrofoam comes in thinner 4' x 8' sheets and can be found at most hardware stores. The cell structure of this Styrofoam is more densely packed and is less messy when cut. Packing Styrofoam pieces can also be recycled from shipping boxes. They come in all sizes, shapes, and thicknesses. These miscellaneous pieces can be glued, sculpted, and attached as 3-D parts or as assembled architectural pieces on larger props. White 4' x 8' Styrofoam sheets come in sizes from ½" to 2" thick and have a larger cell structure. When cut, this crumbly texture can be used purposely to create rough stone edges or a worn prop appearance.

Large, flat pieces of Styrofoam can be cut with a straight edge and scoring. Once the piece is scored, hold one side of the score firmly against a flat surface such as a tabletop, and with your other hand gently push down on the opposite scored side. The Styrofoam will snap apart with a clean, straight edge.

Styrofoam can be made to resemble just about anything. It's lightweight, inexpensive, and easy to work with. It can be used to make everything from small prop tombstones to larger layered structures. Once the basic Styrofoam shape is cut and the design drawn out with a permanent marker, heated tools are then used to shape, cut into, or sculpt the piece further. Do this in a well-ventilated area and take precautions against fumes. As the heated tool is pressed into the Styrofoam, the Styrofoam quickly melts away from the hot edge. Practice on a sample piece first. You will need to work fast, and this could take some practice before you get the hang of it.

Tools:

Various tools can be used to cut and shape Styrofoam. Shown on the right are a battery-operated hot wire cutter, woodburning tools with various tips, a soldering iron, an electric wire-cutting tool, a serrated knife, spray paint, and a heat gun with low setting. Spray paint and a heat gun can both be used to quickly roughen the edges of a Styrofoam prop.

Shown right: spray paint on Styrofoam "eats" away at the material, and a heat gun melts it. Both create a natural worn-edge look. Use either method sparingly and in a well-ventilated area.

Never leave heated tools unattended, and use in a well-ventilated area!

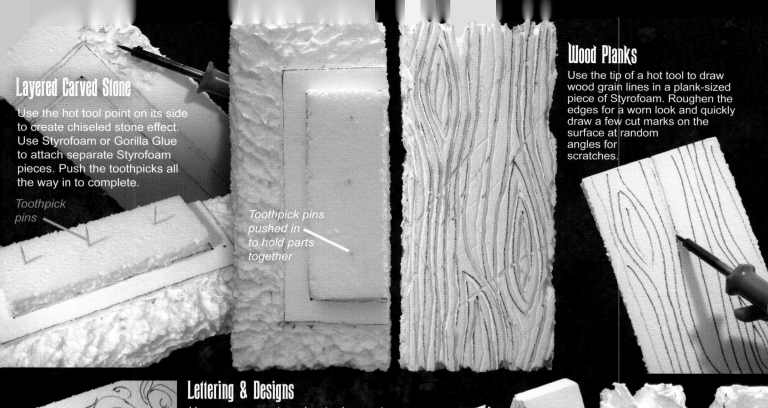

Layered Carved Stone

Use the hot tool point on its side to create chiseled stone effect. Use Styrofoam or Gorilla Glue to attach separate Styrofoam pieces. Push the toothpicks all the way in to complete.

Toothpick pins

Toothpick pins pushed in to hold parts together

Wood Planks

Use the tip of a hot tool to draw wood grain lines in a plank-sized piece of Styrofoam. Roughen the edges for a worn look and quickly draw a few cut marks on the surface at random angles for scratches.

Lettering & Designs

Use a permanent marker to draw out your design. With a hot tool held like a pencil, trace back over the design. Move the tool quickly to make sure too much of the design isn't melted away.

BELOVED

Cracks & Cut Marks

Hold the hot tool against the Styrofoam longer to melt out large cuts or holes. Melt away any sharp or straight edges to create a worn-away effect. For cut marks, start off pushing the tool a little harder into the Styrofoam and then gradually pull up until the tool no longer touches the surface. Do several of these parallel to each other for claw marks.

Crumbling Brick & Plaster

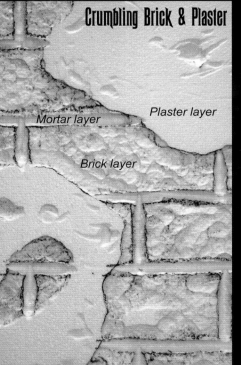

Plaster layer

Mortar layer

Brick layer

There are three levels of this design. The deepest level will be the mortar line between the bricks. *Don't go too deep* or the Styrofoam could break. The midlevel is the brick surface. Use the hot tool to lower it just enough to leave a small edge where the plaster overlaps the brick. Roughen the brick surface with the side of the heated tool tip. The top, highest level, is the plaster. Create some random dent and scratch marks in the surface.

Natural Stone Wall

Draw out some randomly shaped and sized stones. Use the hot tool to lower the mortar between the stones. Further shape the stone edges for a rounder look.

Next Steps:

Once your Styrofoam prop has been completed you can cover the surface with *Monster Mud (page 11)*. When this is dry, it can be painted with craft paints.

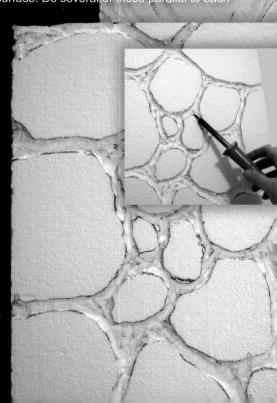

Illuminated Gothic Pillars

YOU WILL NEED, plastic skulls, dowel rods, paper towels, duct tape, 4" PVC pipe cut to desired height, ½" wood for base, a bucket, Monster Mud, white and black paint, tin foil, small battery-operated candles, cardboard scraps, sponge, X-Acto knife, drill, jigsaw cutter, old fabric for strips, craft glue or Mod Podge, wide brush, plastic bag or old rag, old toothbrush, two or more plastic flower pots with separate water base parts, string, hot tool (wood burning tool or soldering iron), hot glue gun and glue sticks, small dowel rod and piece

Create these custom, old stone Gothic pillars to light the path or doorway of this year's home haunt. They use only a few basic materials and are easy to make, so make two or more and light the

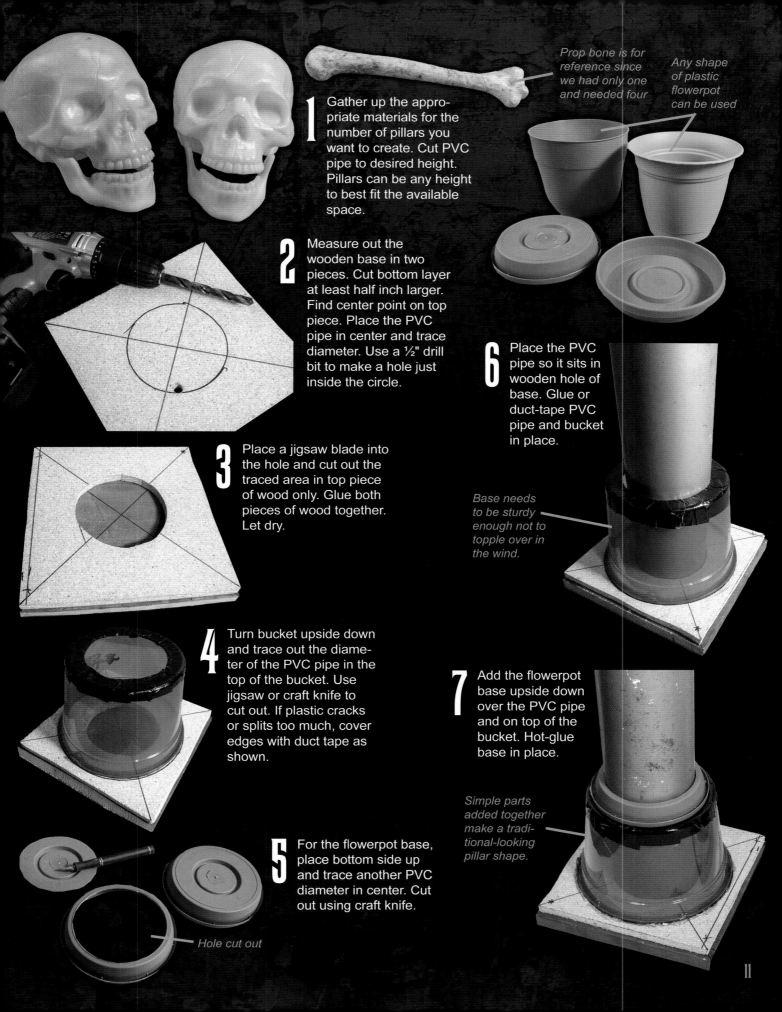

Prop bone is for reference since we had only one and needed four

Any shape of plastic flowerpot can be used

1 Gather up the appropriate materials for the number of pillars you want to create. Cut PVC pipe to desired height. Pillars can be any height to best fit the available space.

2 Measure out the wooden base in two pieces. Cut bottom layer at least half inch larger. Find center point on top piece. Place the PVC pipe in center and trace diameter. Use a ½" drill bit to make a hole just inside the circle.

3 Place a jigsaw blade into the hole and cut out the traced area in top piece of wood only. Glue both pieces of wood together. Let dry.

4 Turn bucket upside down and trace out the diameter of the PVC pipe in the top of the bucket. Use jigsaw or craft knife to cut out. If plastic cracks or splits too much, cover edges with duct tape as shown.

5 For the flowerpot base, place bottom side up and trace another PVC diameter in center. Cut out using craft knife.

Hole cut out

6 Place the PVC pipe so it sits in wooden hole of base. Glue or duct-tape PVC pipe and bucket in place.

Base needs to be sturdy enough not to topple over in the wind.

7 Add the flowerpot base upside down over the PVC pipe and on top of the bucket. Hot-glue base in place.

Simple parts added together make a traditional-looking pillar shape.

8 Using a hot tool (wood-cutting tool or soldering iron), melt some small holes around the edges of two plastic flowerpots. Thread a string through the holes of both, pull tight, and knot. Add another hole to top center flowerpot to fit a dowel rod into.

9 For each plastic skull, cut or melt the eye sections out. Make two small holes on each side of the jaw where it connects to the back of the skull. Tie a string through holes and over jaw hinge to keep the jawbone open all the way. Also, cut a dowel rod hole at base of skull. Last, cut open an access door at back of skull to place candles inside later. Leave one side attached so it can be closed.

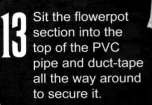

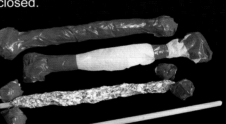

13 Sit the flowerpot section into the top of the PVC pipe and duct-tape all the way around to secure it.

14 Create a 2" cuff out of paper towels for below the top flowerpot and over the PVC connection point. Duct-tape in place.

To create the crossbones:
A. Cut two dowel rods about 13" long. Wrap length in tin foil. Use paper towel to form four small ball shapes and secure with piece of duct tape. **B.** Wrap the length of dowel rod in more paper towels and cover rod and ball shapes in duct tape as shown. Two bones will be needed for each scull. **C.** Finished bones don't have to be perfect or identical.

10

11 Attach the two crossed bones to the dowel rod, one in front and one behind the dowel rod. Attach with duct tape. Keep the skull removable.

12 To create the skull base decoration, roll up some paper towel sections to cover the length of one flowerpot. Each section is bigger at bottom than top. Add enough sections to go all the way around, and secure with more duct tape. Remember this is meant to look like weathered stone, so nothing must be too precise in its shape.

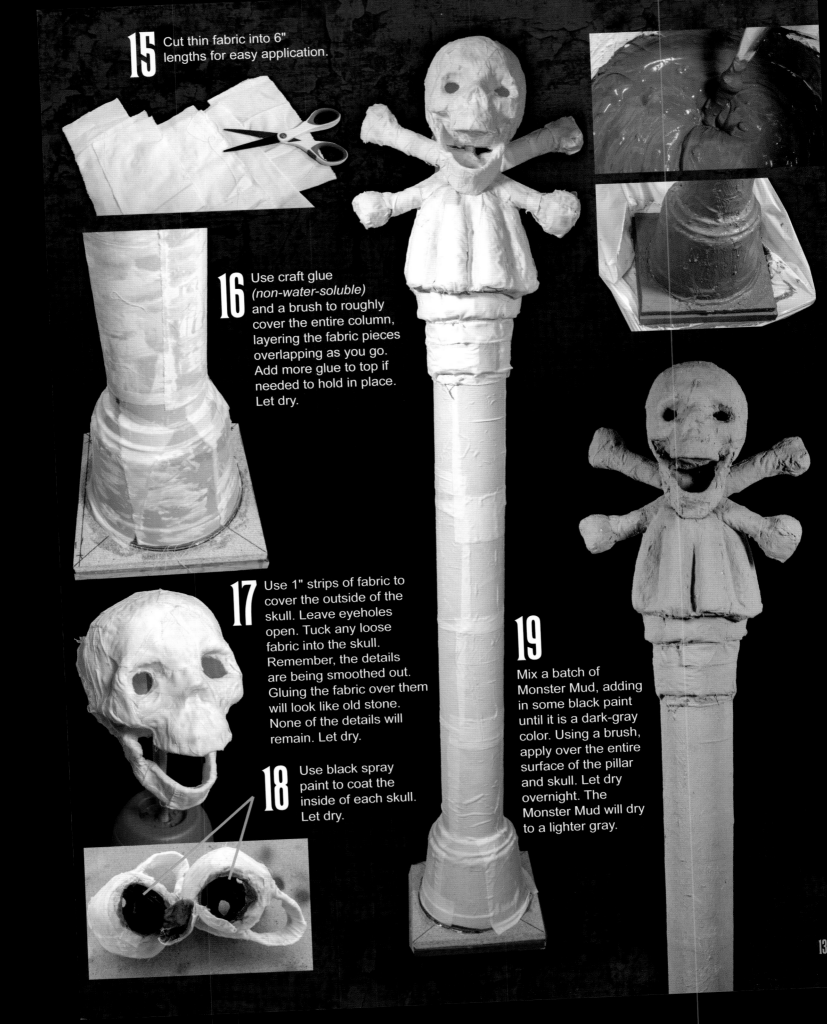

15 Cut thin fabric into 6" lengths for easy application.

16 Use craft glue *(non-water-soluble)* and a brush to roughly cover the entire column, layering the fabric pieces overlapping as you go. Add more glue to top if needed to hold in place. Let dry.

17 Use 1" strips of fabric to cover the outside of the skull. Leave eyeholes open. Tuck any loose fabric into the skull. Remember, the details are being smoothed out. Gluing the fabric over them will look like old stone. None of the details will remain. Let dry.

18 Use black spray paint to coat the inside of each skull. Let dry.

19 Mix a batch of Monster Mud, adding in some black paint until it is a dark-gray color. Using a brush, apply over the entire surface of the pillar and skull. Let dry overnight. The Monster Mud will dry to a lighter gray.

20 Next use a bunched-up plastic bag or rag to apply black paint sporadically over entire surface, letting some of the Monster Mud show through. Use an old toothbrush to get paint into the recessed areas. Let dry.

21 To get a spotty, old-stone look, cut out rough circles on one side of a sponge, using an X-Acto knife.

22 Mix a small batch of Monster Mud to a light-gray to white color. Do not mix the colors completely, keeping a marbled appearance.

23 Dip the sponge into the Monster Mud and dab onto the raised column surface areas. Do not over-apply. Leave some of the previous colors showing through.

Don't forget to apply Monster Mud on the bottom underneath of the pillar to weatherproof it!

Cardboard pieces

24 To create a simple base for the candles to sit on, cut out two pieces of 1.5" squares in cardboard. Cut out a hole for a dowel rod to fit into. Next, cut out two 3.5" long pieces of cardboard wide enough for the candles to sit on. Hot-glue the larger stacks onto the smaller stacks.

25 Trim the skull dowel rod if needed, so that the candle platform can be inserted on it and sit flat inside the skull. Do not permanently attach to skull if you want to keep it removable.

Skull Clasp

26 **To create the skull clasp:** Use a small dowel rod or stick about 2" long. Twist a wire along the center of the wood, then twist the two ends together. Insert the wire into a hole near the opening at the back of the skull. Bend the wire inside the skull so that the wood handle can be turned to hold the skull door closed. Wrap black duct tape on the stick ends if it needs more padding to hold the door closed.

Skull clasp

27 *Use only battery-operated candles inside this prop!* Two candles placed inside the skull will light up both the eyes nicely at night.

Inside the Coffin
Getting the Best Eternal Sleep Ever!

YOU WILL NEED: wooden prop coffin with lid, L brackets, wooden trim for lid, oval picture frame, two handles, small door hinges, staple gun, 5/16" staples, white cotton or silk fabric that has been dyed a grungy color, needle and thread, bag of Poly-fil, wing nut and bolt, two 1" washers, black and brown paint, drill, screws, jigsaw, toothbrush, strong wood glue, hot-glue gun and sticks, coffin prop figure, LED light or flashlight (optional)

E ven the dead want to look their best on Halloween! Turn a plain wooden coffin prop into a high-class viewing coffin with padded interior. Whether it's fancy new satins or slightly stained and used fabrics, your occupants will love the attention to detail.

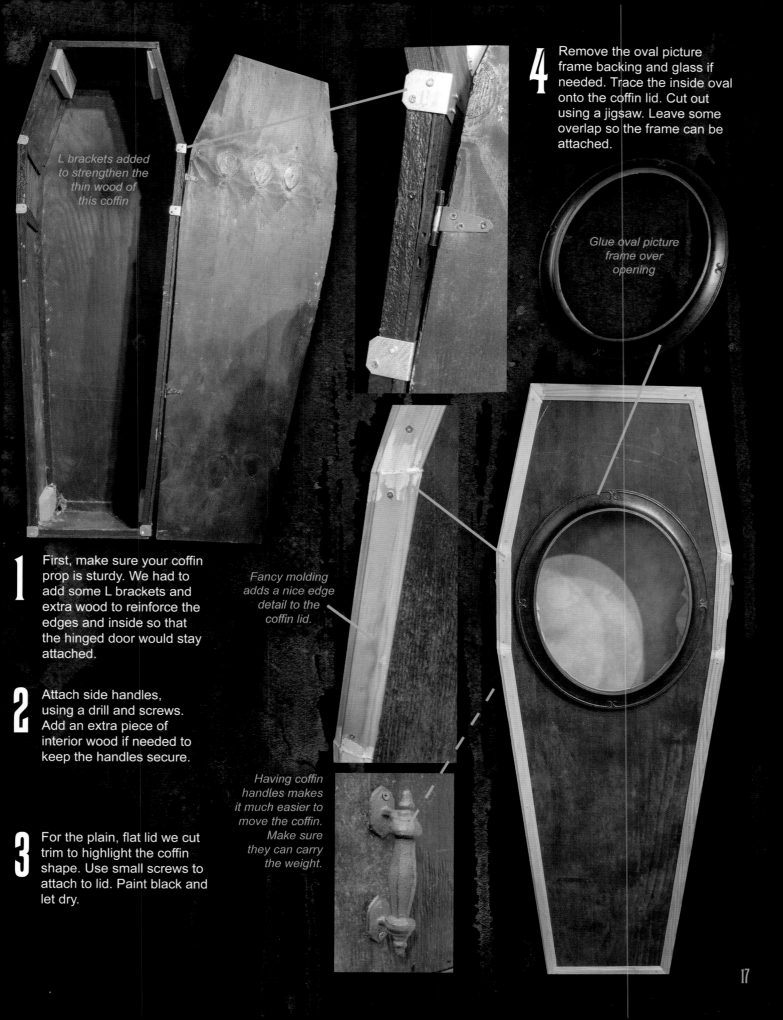

L brackets added to strengthen the thin wood of this coffin

4 Remove the oval picture frame backing and glass if needed. Trace the inside oval onto the coffin lid. Cut out using a jigsaw. Leave some overlap so the frame can be attached.

Glue oval picture frame over opening

1 First, make sure your coffin prop is sturdy. We had to add some L brackets and extra wood to reinforce the edges and inside so that the hinged door would stay attached.

Fancy molding adds a nice edge detail to the coffin lid.

2 Attach side handles, using a drill and screws. Add an extra piece of interior wood if needed to keep the handles secure.

Having coffin handles makes it much easier to move the coffin. Make sure they can carry the weight.

3 For the plain, flat lid we cut trim to highlight the coffin shape. Use small screws to attach to lid. Paint black and let dry.

17

5

Cut out one length of fabric to fit the coffin interior back and one length to fit the interior sides. This portion will be completely hidden, so it can be scrap fabric.

6

Line the inside bottom of the coffin with Poly-fil. Place the centered fabric over the Poly-fil and staple around the back edges to keep in place. Leave the fabric a little loose so it forms a bit of a pillow for the back. Do the same thing for each of the interior coffin sides. Tuck the top edge of fabric below the front edge to allow the lid to still close flat.

7

Measure out another length of dyed fabric for the interior sides. Double the length needed. Leave at least 2" over all the way around and cut. Use a needle and thread to loosely stitch across the top so a gather can be pulled. Do the same for bottom edge. Make sure you have enough length to cover the sides.

8

Staple this to the edges of the interior coffin, leaving the gathered center loose and puffy over the poly-filled portion. Staple along edge at the back of coffin.

After dyeing the fabric, the fabric was bunched up and left to dry so that it would stay wrinkled for a nice aged effect.

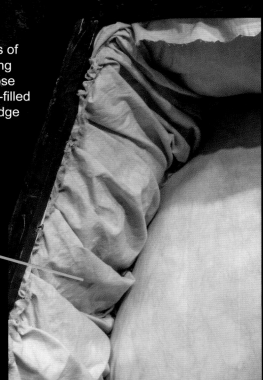

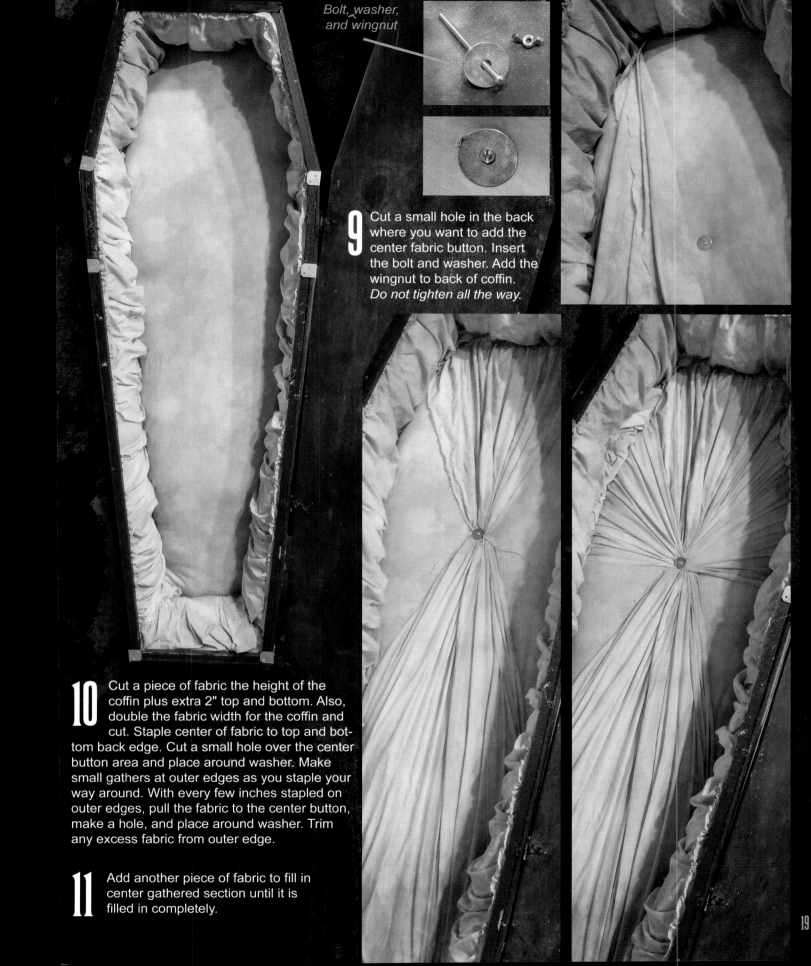

Bolt, washer, and wingnut

9 Cut a small hole in the back where you want to add the center fabric button. Insert the bolt and washer. Add the wingnut to back of coffin. *Do not tighten all the way.*

10 Cut a piece of fabric the height of the coffin plus extra 2" top and bottom. Also, double the fabric width for the coffin and cut. Staple center of fabric to top and bottom back edge. Cut a small hole over the center button area and place around washer. Make small gathers at outer edges as you staple your way around. With every few inches stapled on outer edges, pull the fabric to the center button, make a hole, and place around washer. Trim any excess fabric from outer edge.

11 Add another piece of fabric to fill in center gathered section until it is filled in completely.

Fabric-covered
center button

12 Use second washer to create a fabric-covered button. Add a small piece of Poly-fil to washer top. Cover with fabric and close with a few stitches, using a needle and thread. Trim excess fabric. Sew or hot-glue over first washer button.

13 Add the coffin prop figure. We used a skeletal bride here. *TIP:* Interior looks great when lit from inside with an LED light or flashlight.

14 For a coffin without viewing window, add some silk fabric, using same method as interior base, gathering at center point. Interior excess fabric can be trimmed to hang over at stapled edges as longer, rough-cut ruffles for a creepy look. Watered-down brown paint can be sprayed onto the fabric for an aged look. A toothbrush and black paint can be used to add moldy spots.

Quick & Dirty Sand-Casting

For a Realistic Cast-Iron Look

If you need a quick and easy way to cast small objects for use in the haunted house, this method of sand-casting is just what you need. Hot glue is used to fill the sand impressions, and its grainy, imperfect surface texture will resemble cast iron when painted black. Keep in mind that you will be casting only a side of your object, not the entire three-dimensional surface. You should be able to press the object into the sand and pull it back out.

A cemetery fence pole topper is being cast here from a metal object. To start, fill a large enough container to cast your piece, which is at least 2" deep. The sand should be slightly moist but not wet. Use a spray bottle to mist the sand if it dries out.

YOU WILL NEED: two or more bags of hot-glue sticks, hot-glue gun, black craft paint or spray paint for finishing, one bag of paver sand, large enough container for casting object/s, casting object, spoon handle, X-Acto knife

Firmly press your object into the sand. Press the object in as far as possible, but not so deep that the sand covers the object. If needed, create the 1" long stem that will later slip into a PVC fence post. A spoon handle end works well here.

Gently wiggle the object from side to side to pack the sand on the sides. Very carefully lift the object straight out. You can use your finger to pat any fallen sand back into place.

Some castings with lots of detail work best being filled by a glue gun. If you are interrupted or need to take a break, you can always resume filling more hot glue on top of already dried glue.

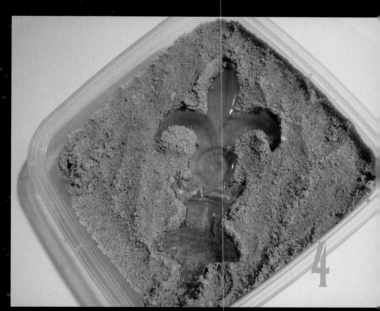

Hot glue *is HOT!* Do not let it touch any skin or delicate materials. A good safety tip is to keep a bowl of water with ice cubes nearby in case you get hot glue on your skin. Immediately dip the skin in the ice water to instantly cool the glue. Let casting cool completely.

Once it's removed from sand, brush any loose sand away. Make sure the casting is dry, then spray-paint black.

Test the fence topper for fit in the PVC pole. You may need to add or subtract some of the stem. Use an X-Acto to trim excess away or use a glue gun to add more stem width if needed. It should be a snug fit into the pole, yet still removable.

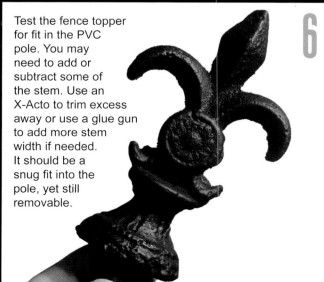

Dripping Candles

L ight up your haunted house with these reusable, safe candles. These candles look as if they have been burning all night, dripping faux waxy trails down the sides and pooling at the candle base. Add candleholders or candelabras, or just leave freestanding in a variety of shapes and sizes. *As a bonus . . .* these hot-glue candles glow in the dark when used with a black light!

Grouping of different-size candles, or candles placed at different heights using a mismatched series of candleholders, is a great look for the haunted house or graveyard.

YOU WILL NEED: straight PVC pipe connection pieces in various sizes or a PVC tube that has been cut into various sizes, X-Acto knife, flickering tea lights, hot-glue gun, two or more bags of hot-glue sticks, 2" thick Styrofoam pieces cut out to fit into the PVC pieces, bowl of ice cubes (to help cool down hot-glue quickly), serrated knife, marker, wax paper, candle stands *(optional)*

Place wax paper underneath before starting, so the hot glue does not stick to the wax paper.

*Remove tea light **before** adding hot glue.*

1

Firmly press the PVC piece into a sheet of Styrofoam to make an impression. Use a serrated knife to cut out the circle. Next, position a tea light in the center and trace around edge with a marker. Use an X-Acto to cut out the space without going all the way through, so that the tea light can sit inside.

2

Press the Styrofoam piece into the PVC candle. Place a sheet of wax paper under the candle. Begin applying hot glue to the candle top and sides, mimicking the way a real melted candle would look.

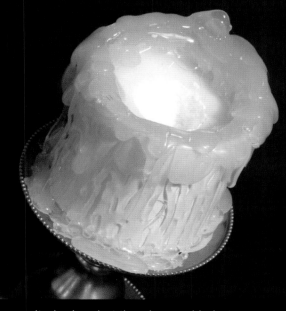

3

Build up the top melted edge. Let the glue cool in between layers to help build height.

4

Sample of PVC pipe that has been cut on an angle for the top candle ends

One way to help build height is to hold the freshly glued PVC upside down over a bowl of ice cubes. Keep PVC moving so the glue does not run off the PVC.

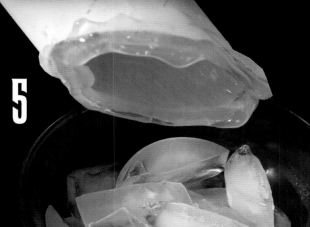

5

For the bottom edge of candles without candleholders, let the hot glue pool at the base. Place wax paper underneath before starting; since the hot glue does not stick to the wax paper, it will be easy to remove. The tea lights should remain removable for easy access to turn on and change the batteries when needed.

6

Ancient Reliquary
Vampire Queen Relic

YOU WILL NEED: plastic skull; large glass and metal lantern that the skull will sit in; marker; cardboard; red velvet fabric; hot tool; scrap Styrofoam; tin foil; small wires; oven-bake modeling clay; X-Acto knife; superglue; yellow, brown, black, and white craft paint; black wig with long hair; various beads, necklaces, or other jewels; paper and ink; dowel rod; string; serrated knife; spray glue; wire cutters; hot-glue gun and glue sticks

This ancient vampire queen's head was removed sometime in the 18th century and placed as a treasured relic in this glass case. Be it a library curiosity or a mantelpiece focal point, this macabre relic is sure to mesmerize your guests!

1 This skull didn't quite fit inside the display case we had, so we cut off some of the back of the skull.

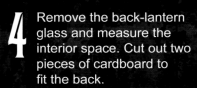

2 Mark the cut point with marker and cut with a serrated knife. Use a hot tool to add a hole for the dowel rod at the base of the skull.

4 Remove the back-lantern glass and measure the interior space. Cut out two pieces of cardboard to fit the back.

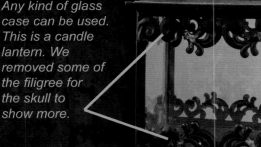

Any kind of glass case can be used. This is a candle lantern. We removed some of the filigree for the skull to show more.

3 Using a hot tool, carefully melt away the teeth of the plastic skull. Add a few holes to insert new teeth into for the top and bottom jaws. Doesn't have to be too many. Relics tend to lose a few pieces over the centuries.

5 Cut a piece of fabric to cover the board with 1" extra overhang. Spray glue on the boards and attach the velvet fabric to the front. Turn edges to back and glue in place. Paint the second board black on one side.

6 Glue the backside of the fabric panel and attach backside of black painted board together.

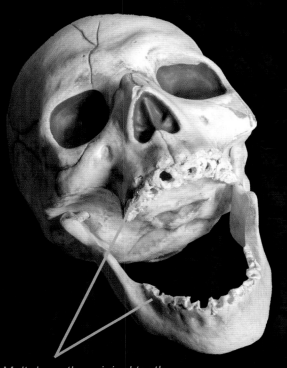

7 Measure the bottom of the display case. Create another fabric-covered panel and insert into case bottom. To support the skull and keep it in place, cut a piece of Styrofoam that will fit below the skull. Insert a dowel rod in center. Cover the Styrofoam with more fabric and spray-glue in place.

Melt down the original teeth and make holes for new teeth. The melted plastic will add to the worn bone look once painted.

Skull support

27

8 Cut a short wire for each tooth. Use modeling clay to create the rough shape of teeth, including two fangs with a wire in center of each. Make a tooth stem that can insert into the tooth hole. These teeth are meant to be old and worn, so they don't have to be perfect. Insert each tooth wire into some tinfoil to keep them upright and separated. Bake in oven according to clay instructions.

9 Once the teeth have cooled, clip the wire shorter to fit into tooth hole of the jaw. Super-glue each tooth into place. Some holes can be left empty. Gaps between teeth also look good. Let dry.

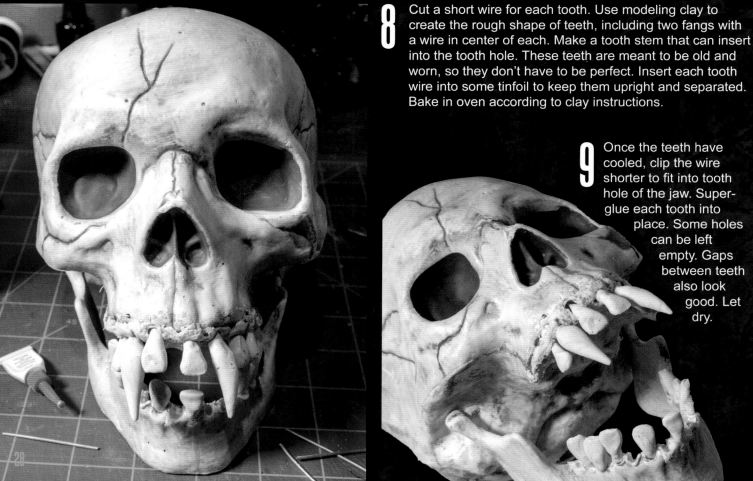

10 Paint entire skull, teeth, and jaw, except inner eye and nose holes, with yellow craft paint. Let dry.

11 Next, using a dark-brown craft paint, brush on a small amount of paint and dab with a rag or your hand to pull some of the paint back off. Some of the yellow should still be visible. A grunge effect is the goal here. Paint entire skull, teeth, and jaw. Let dry.

12 Use black craft paint to high-light areas, letting some of the original paint show through. Also paint the recessed areas around each tooth and the inside of the jaw.

13 Last, add a small number of white highlights where the bone might naturally wear down the most. Also, add a wash of white over the teeth color. Let dry.

14 Cut some long strands of wig hair and add a small amount of hot glue to ends and stick to skull top. *BE CAREFUL!* The hot glue will melt the hair strands quickly, so don't hold it too close to the glued area. The hair here is also used to cover the back of the skull that was cut so it would fit in the case.

15 Use any color of jewels, beads, or metal pieces to create a crown to sit around the skull forehead. Here, we also added four long strands of beads to hang down the sides.

16 A small scrap of paper was stained with a wash of paint and crumpled up several times for aging to create the display tag and show the hand-written vampire queen's name or history.

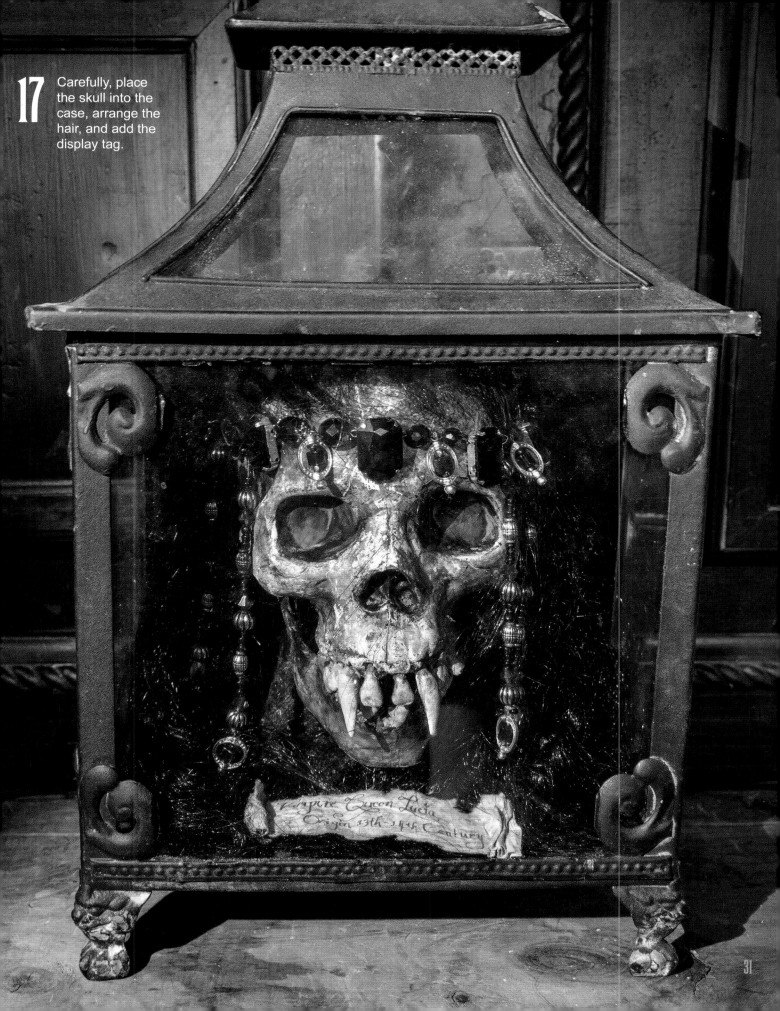

17 Carefully, place the skull into the case, arrange the hair, and add the display tag.

Vampire Cyren Lucia
Origin 13th-14th Century

Bringing a Ghost to Life
Pepper's Ghost Using a Prop

YOU WILL NEED: a standing or suspended figure prop with white details that show up in blacklight; a sheet of Plexiglas large enough to reflect the prop; some black material or black plastic for a backdrop; a black light; a second light source *(does not have to be a black light)*; props or scene placed behind the glass; some cord to suspend the prop; a ceiling hook

This version of a Pepper's Ghost can be used indoors or out. Position the prop in front of a black background. Place one or more black lights to the side or bottom of the prop so they do not have a reflection in the glass. The glass should be at a 45-degree angle to the prop and placed so the viewers can look through the glass and see the reflected prop. Other props or structures should conceal the prop and the black light. Behind the glass, place more props or a scene setup for the "ghost" to appear in front of. A second light source should be positioned to light the scene but not shine on the glass itself. Use a fence or obstacle to keep the viewers at a distance to the glass and keep the hidden prop out of sight.

In the Cemetery

Suspended prop is hidden behind a large prop. Put black fabric or black plastic behind the prop and on the sides if needed. Point some black lights at the prop but positioned so they don't show in the glass. Position the sheet of glass so it is at a 45-degree angle to the prop, either right or left of the prop. Use stakes in front and behind the edges of the glass to hold it up. Use other strategically placed props or tree branches to conceal the stakes. You should be able to see the reflected prop in the center of the glass if standing in the viewer's position *(usually behind a fence or obstruction)*. The goal is to control the angle the viewer will see the effect and how far away they will be from the glass.

Tip: It is dangerous to use real glass in a Pepper's Ghost effect. Someone could walk into it or break it. Plexiglas works just fine. Make sure you have a secure way of supporting it. Keep in mind that the wind may blow against it and could knock it down. Make sturdy supports wherever possible.

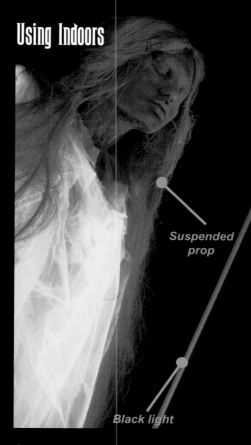

Suspended prop

Black light

Shown here: Stairs are cordoned off with haunt warning tape. A door-sized piece of Plexiglas is placed on an angle at the top of the stairs in a doorway. Prop is suspended from the ceiling in a small alcove at the top of the stairs to the right. A black light is positioned on both sides of the prop, concealed from reflection, with more black cloth suspended from the ceiling.

Ghost reflection

Glass on angle

Black light

In the room behind the glass, a sound-activated lamp turns on and off as the sound of a woman mournfully crying plays on a CD player. This causes a viewer to look up the stairs and in the direction of the Pepper's Ghost effect.

The Drinking Ghoul

with an Unending Thirst

T his drinking ghoul cannot satisfy its undead thirst. The liquid keeps on pouring and the ghoul keeps on drinking. He appears to have just crawled up out of a grave. A tattered, dirty shirt conceals the ghoul's bucket "body." One arm reveals a skeleton bone. In a shrunken hand is the bottle it cannot put down.

YOU WILL NEED: one plastic bottle with long neck, a small pond pump, a bucket, a prop skull head, paper towels, carpet glue, rubber tubing, an old shirt, a prop arm bone, craft paints, hot-glue gun, glue sticks, 1" x 2" wood pieces cut to size, wood screws, pipe installation tubing, long neck funnel, scissors, X-Acto knife, duct tape, one poseable prop hand (or make one with wires and hot glue), L brackets, zip ties

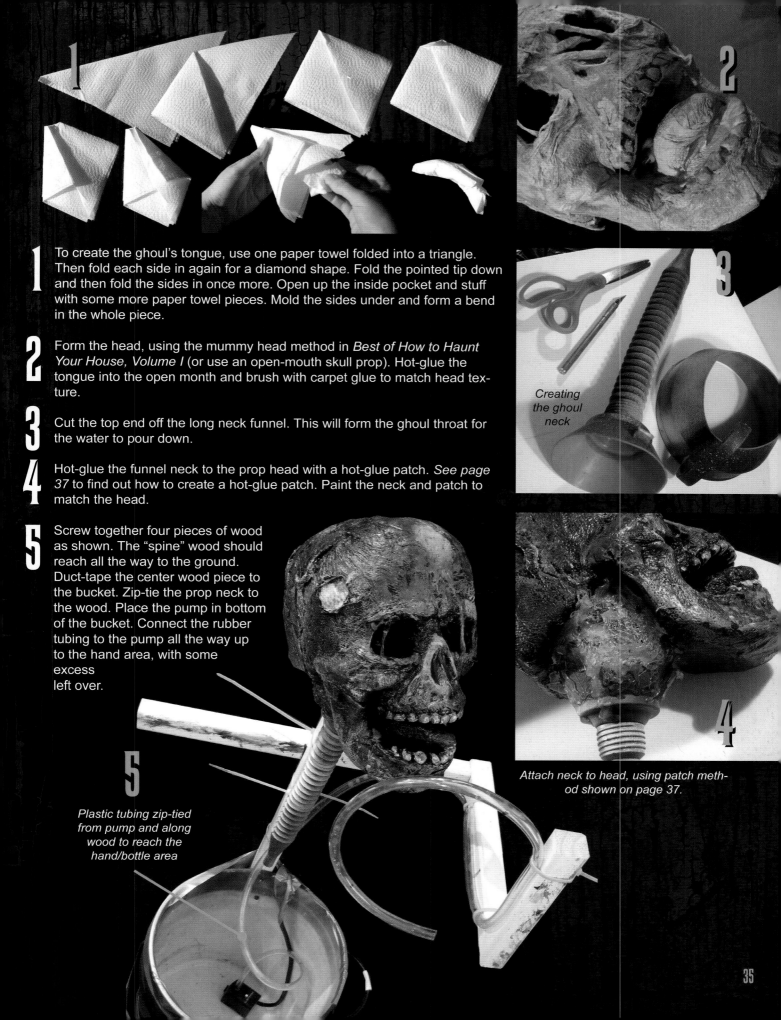

1 To create the ghoul's tongue, use one paper towel folded into a triangle. Then fold each side in again for a diamond shape. Fold the pointed tip down and then fold the sides in once more. Open up the inside pocket and stuff with some more paper towel pieces. Mold the sides under and form a bend in the whole piece.

2 Form the head, using the mummy head method in *Best of How to Haunt Your House, Volume I* (or use an open-mouth skull prop). Hot-glue the tongue into the open month and brush with carpet glue to match head texture.

3 Cut the top end off the long neck funnel. This will form the ghoul throat for the water to pour down.

4 Hot-glue the funnel neck to the prop head with a hot-glue patch. *See page 37* to find out how to create a hot-glue patch. Paint the neck and patch to match the head.

5 Screw together four pieces of wood as shown. The "spine" wood should reach all the way to the ground. Duct-tape the center wood piece to the bucket. Zip-tie the prop neck to the wood. Place the pump in bottom of the bucket. Connect the rubber tubing to the pump all the way up to the hand area, with some excess left over.

Creating the ghoul neck

Attach neck to head, using patch method shown on page 37.

5

Plastic tubing zip-tied from pump and along wood to reach the hand/bottle area

6 Attach the poseable hand to the wood, using wood screws. Cut a hole in the plastic bottle. Run the plastic tubing into the bottle and seal around the hole opening with hot glue. Hot-glue the prop fingers to the bottle.

7 Adjust the arm and head angle and secure with duct tape or screws.

8 Put an old shirt on the figure. Cut open the shirt arm on the side and hot-glue a prop arm bone just inside the opening.

Don't forget to add some dramatic lighting!

Add some glow-in-the-dark paint to the skull eyes for a scarier look. Paint the pupils with black.

Add a creative bottle label of your choice before attaching hand.

Add some hot-glue drool drippings to the mouth, using the Dripping Candle method on page 24.

Grunge up the shirt with some black and brown craft paint.

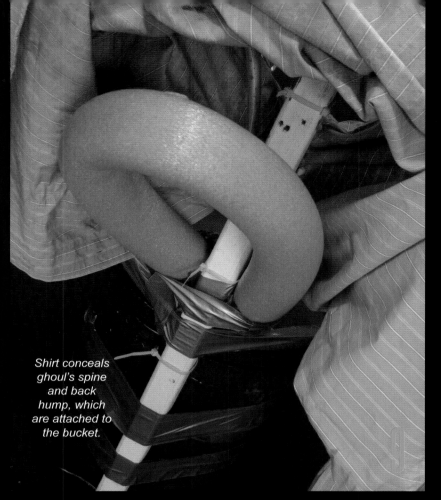

Shirt conceals ghoul's spine and back hump, which are attached to the bucket.

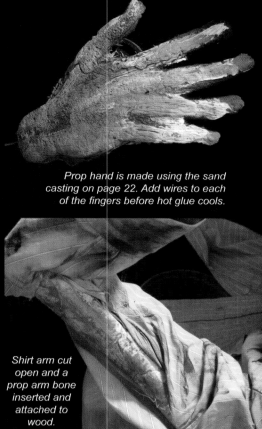

Prop hand is made using the sand casting on page 22. Add wires to each of the fingers before hot glue cools.

Shirt arm cut open and a prop arm bone inserted and attached to wood.

9 To help fill out the figure's back, attach a bent piece of installation tubing to the spine and duct-tape in place.

10 When placing the figure in the haunt setting, open the shirt so the water will run into the bucket. Place the tombstones or other props around figure to hide the bucket.

11 Fill the bucket with enough water to cover the pond pump. Turn pump on to test. Make any adjustments needed for the liquid to pour from the bottle into the mouth and from the mouth into the bucket.

Plastic tube is run up the arm along the wood and inserted into bottle.

Making a Hot-Glue Patch

Use a hot-glue gun and a bowl of water. Use the hot-glue gun to draw a series of overlapping circles over the water. Then draw random swirls of hot glue to fill in the patch. When the glue is cool, remove from the water. This can be used to fill a large open area of hot glue on props or as an interesting texture to be applied to all sorts of other projects. Paint as needed.

2

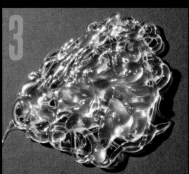

3

Making Your Own
Tombstone
with Double Columns

Ayatha & Christie

How
They Died
Is Still
A Mystery...

YOU WILL NEED: one cutout 2" thick Styrofoam tombstone *(4' x 4')*; one cutout 2" thick Styrofoam book row *(1' x 4')*; carbon paper; enlarged template design or freehand-drawn text template; ballpoint pen; black permanent marker; hot cutting tools of choice; serrated knife; Monster Mud *(page 7)*; black, brown, and white craft paints *(or colors of choice)*; paintbrushes; sponge; cheesecloth or makeup wedge for applying paint; two garden statues *(see page 42)* or urns with faux flowers for columns; one cardboard building-form tube cut in half; two Styrofoam tortilla containers *(lid will not be used)*; two square-cut pieces of Styrofoam *(for column bases)*; two lengths of pool noodle sections or round pipe insulation *(for ring at base of column)*; toothpicks; Gorilla Glue; latex gloves

TIP: Light large tombstones from the ground, pointing up for an extra eerie look. A round shop light with blue bulb was used here. Throw in a couple of creepy dolls and the look is complete. Visit www.howtohauntyourhouse.com for information on making these dolls.

Large tombstones are a great focal point in the home-haunt cemetery. Two columns, each topped with a faux metal statue, flank this tombstone project. If statues aren't available, other props such as urns and faux flowers could be used. The columns could also be used on their own or used inside the haunted house.

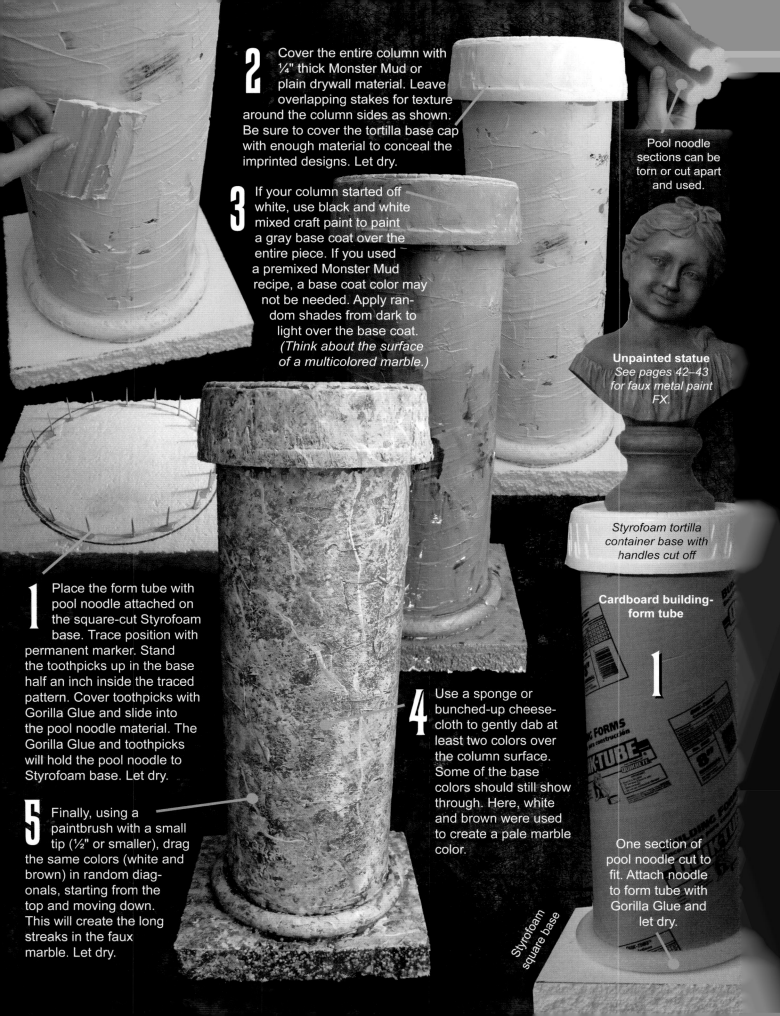

2 Cover the entire column with ¼" thick Monster Mud or plain drywall material. Leave overlapping stakes for texture around the column sides as shown. Be sure to cover the tortilla base cap with enough material to conceal the imprinted designs. Let dry.

3 If your column started off white, use black and white mixed craft paint to paint a gray base coat over the entire piece. If you used a premixed Monster Mud recipe, a base coat color may not be needed. Apply random shades from dark to light over the base coat. *(Think about the surface of a multicolored marble.)*

Pool noodle sections can be torn or cut apart and used.

Unpainted statue
See pages 42–43 for faux metal paint FX.

Styrofoam tortilla container base with handles cut off

Cardboard building-form tube

1 Place the form tube with pool noodle attached on the square-cut Styrofoam base. Trace position with permanent marker. Stand the toothpicks up in the base half an inch inside the traced pattern. Cover toothpicks with Gorilla Glue and slide into the pool noodle material. The Gorilla Glue and toothpicks will hold the pool noodle to Styrofoam base. Let dry.

4 Use a sponge or bunched-up cheese-cloth to gently dab at least two colors over the column surface. Some of the base colors should still show through. Here, white and brown were used to create a pale marble color.

1

One section of pool noodle cut to fit. Attach noodle to form tube with Gorilla Glue and let dry.

5 Finally, using a paintbrush with a small tip (½" or smaller), drag the same colors (white and brown) in random diagonals, starting from the top and moving down. This will create the long streaks in the faux marble. Let dry.

Styrofoam square base

6 The Styrofoam tombstone is created from two pieces: the curved back headstone and the row of books along the bottom. With a serrated knife, cut a piece of 2" thick Styrofoam sheet down to 4' x 4'. Cut another piece 1' x 4' for the book row. Cut a curved top on main piece like this one.

See pages 42–43 for faux metal paint FX on statues.

Agatha & Christie

How They Died Is Still A Mystery...

For an extra layer of detail, use a brush to add diluted craft paint drips in brown. Let the paint run down the large cracks and column sides. This just adds another bit of wear and tear. Faux moss can also be applied as shown here. See *Best of How to Haunt Your House, Volume I,* for more information on creating this effect.

7 Freehand-form various thicknesses of book spines on the 1' x 4' piece of Styrofoam as shown.

8 Along the top edge, draw a curve for each book top. Use hot tools to create the details in the Styrofoam. If you have a round, flat-tipped hot tool nib, this works well for pushing in the area along the top. Other nibs can also be used to press the Styrofoam down.

9 Hot tools melt Styrofoam quickly. Don't stay too long in any area. Always practice on a scrap piece of Styrofoam until you get the hang of it. Use a pointed hot tool to create the rest of the book details.

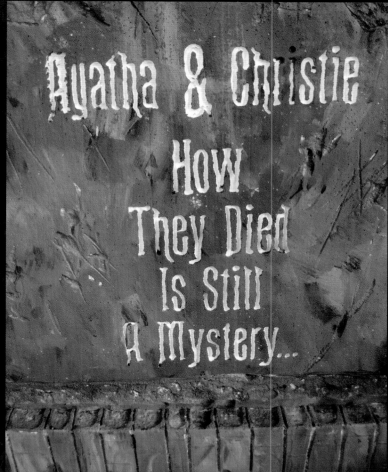

10 Use carbon paper and a ballpoint pen to trace out your tombstone text from a template, or use permanent marker to freehand a design. Use hot tools to push in the letters, cracks, and dents along the edge of the tombstone. Use Gorilla Glue to affix book row to the main tombstone. Let dry.

11 Cover the entire tombstone with Monster Mud *(see page 7).* Let dry. Use black and white craft paints applied loosely with a large paintbrush or sponge to further darken the base color. Let dry.

12 Using a small brush, apply black craft paint into all the letters, cracks, and pushed-in details of the tombstone.

Next, apply similar colors, as used on the columns, with a sponge or cheesecloth. Let dry.

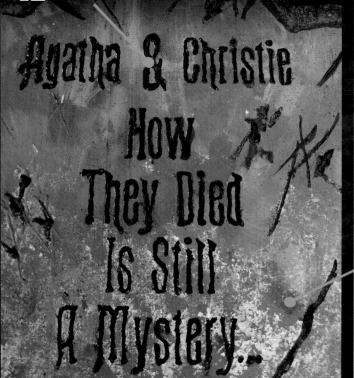

Paint details close-up

Painting Faux Metal

Ancient, weather-worn statues can add a layer of authenticity to the home-haunt, both inside and out. The process uses only paint to transform every-day statuary into haunt-worthy accessories!

1 This statue was purchased at a home design center and was originally made for garden statuary. First, paint the entire piece with either metallic spray paint or brush-applied metallic craft paint. Let dry.

2 Using a sponge, makeup sponge, or bunched-up cheesecloth, gently dab a mixture of dark-green and black craft paint over the surface of the statue. Leave some of the metal paint showing through. Let dry.

Original Statue

YOU WILL NEED: black, white, dark- and light-green craft paints *(or colors of choice);* metallic spray paint or metallic brush-on paint of your choice; paintbrushes; sponge, cheesecloth, or makeup wedge for applying paint; garden statuary prop

3 Mix some dark green and light-green craft paint with a good amount of water. Use a paintbrush to dab along the top of the statute *(in this case, along the hairline works best)* so that the paint runs down the statue. Do this until you have paint drips all around the statue. Try not to disturb the wet paint trails too much. Let them dry completely before moving to the next step.

4 Sparingly, dab a medium or light green on the highest points of the statue. In this case, paint around the dress edge, the base, and the highest points of the hair. This adds a faux corrosive look to the metal.

Completed statue

Applying Paint
You can use a variety of methods to apply paint: with cheesecloth, a paintbrush, or a sponge.

– with cheesecloth

– with a paintbrush

– or with a sponge

Bride's Tomb
Creating a Large-Scale Prop

YOU WILL NEED: 1" x 2" wood, L brackets, wood screws, 2" thick Styrofoam, ¾" Styrofoam, Monster Mud, craft paints, fabric strips, toothpicks, paintbrush, serrated knife, two hinges, ½" PVC poles cut to size, PVC cutter, drill with ⅞" drill bit, duct tape, hot-glue gun, glue sticks, black spray paint

The best thing about large-scale props in your home-haunt setting is their usefulness. You can put things in them, hide things behind them, or cover up parts you don't want to be seen. They also help fill out a setting quickly and make it seem more realistic by having a variety of structure sizes. One of the most important things to keep in mind is how it will be disassembled and stored once the event is over. It's unlikely family members will want to look at a mausoleum all year long in the backyard, and the family dog may get a complex if forced to live in this new doghouse . . . so a little planning ahead can go a long way. You will want some type of framework and a way to attach and remove the Styrofoam walls easily.

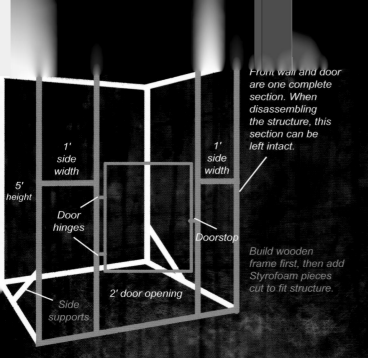

5' height

1' side width

1' side width

Front wall and door are one complete section. When disassembling the structure, this section can be left intact.

Door hinges

Doorstop

Side supports

2' door opening

Build wooden frame first, then add Styrofoam pieces cut to fit structure.

A front stone step inscribed with the word "Beloved" is placed on top of some skulls.

1 First determine the approximate size the structure will be. Sheets of Styrofoam are 4' x 8'. Keeping the depth of your structure 4' or less and no more than 8' high would make things easier. Create a front wall and door section as shown above. Add a simple box frame to this section, using L brackets and wood screws. Use two more lengths of wood to create a door opening at the front. Screw side support pieces at an angle to keep the structure from shifting.

Inside the mausoleum is a painted box that has been topped with a piece of Styrofoam for a small crypt.

2 **Door assembly:** The door should fit inside the front opening with some space free on both sides, to allow for it to open. Drill ⅞" holes along the top and bottom of the doorframe, spaced out. Cut slightly different lengths of ½" PVC pole to create bars. Hot-glue the poles in place. Spray-paint entire door black. Let dry. Attach doorframe to one side of mausoleum front with two hinges. A piece of scrap wood was added to the opposite side as a doorstop to keep the door from swinging in.

Styrofoam walls and ceiling attached with fabric ties

3 Create Styrofoam parts *(see pages 46–47 for construction)* and use fabric ties to attach the Styrofoam to the wooden structure.

4 If using a crypt inside, place a cardboard box in center of the room. Cover with a piece of Styrofoam for a crypt top. Create a second piece to cover the box front.

Front wall and door are one complete section. When disassembling the structure, this section can be left intact.

5 Detail all the walls with a hot tool, using the same methods described on *pages 8–9*. Create cracks, scratches, dents, or wording to complete the look of your structure.

6 Once all the pieces have been Monster Mudded and are dry, paint the whole structure with craft paints, using the same method as on the tombstones *(see page 38)*.

Constructing the Styrofoam Parts

[Ea]ch of the three bride's tomb walls has a separate base. [Th]e base is made from 2" thick Styrofoam. On each end, [ins]ert a 24" fabric strap in two cut double slits, which will [be] used to tie the piece to the wooden structure. Before [cut]ting the slits, cover the spot with a piece of duct tape [on] both the front and back of the Styrofoam. This will help [rein]force the area when the fabric strap is inserted.

[On] top of the base will sit the wall. The wall is made using [1"]Styrofoam. On top of this piece is added two side edge [lay]ers of ¾" Styrofoam. Create several 2¾" thick Sty-[rof]oam bricks in random places. At each corner, insert a [fabr]ic strap, using the method described. Leave the ends [loo]se on the back of the wall. Attach all wall pieces, using [toot]hpicks and craft glue. Let dry. *Note that the back wall of [the] structure can be left plain if it will not be visible.*

Create two smaller side walls for the front of the struc-ture. These will fit on either side of the door. Be sure to leave enough space for the door to open. Start with a layer of ¾" Styrofoam to form a shallow "L" shape for the right-side panel. Mirror this for the left side pan-el. Create a 2" thick Styrofoam base, using the same height as the side walls. Glue this base piece to the layer. Create two side strips of ¾" Styrofoam and glue down. Create the fabric strip openings near each corner and insert the fabric for each.

Over the two front side walls will be a simple length of Styrofoam as a cap. It is attached horizontally over the side front panels by using toothpicks. This makes it easy to remove.

The roof is a piece of 4' width of Styrofoam that is longer than the structure. It should overhang the front by around 6". Where the piece rests on the wooden structure, place a fabric strip for each of the corners. This will tie the roof to the wooden frame.

Roof

Front cap will [sit] horizontally acr[oss] both front side w[alls]

Brick details of various thicknesses

6" h x 4' w front cap

Side wall

Wall base

Cut two vertical slits for fabric ties to insert.

Fabric Ties

Fabric ties are used to hold the Styrofoam to the wooden structure. Cover the Styrofoam area with duct tape, front and back, and make two cuts with a serrated knife for a fabric strip to pass through. Paint over any tie parts that show on the outside.

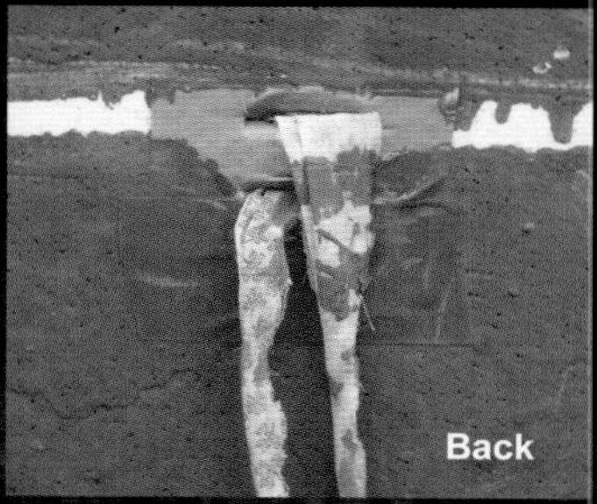

Back

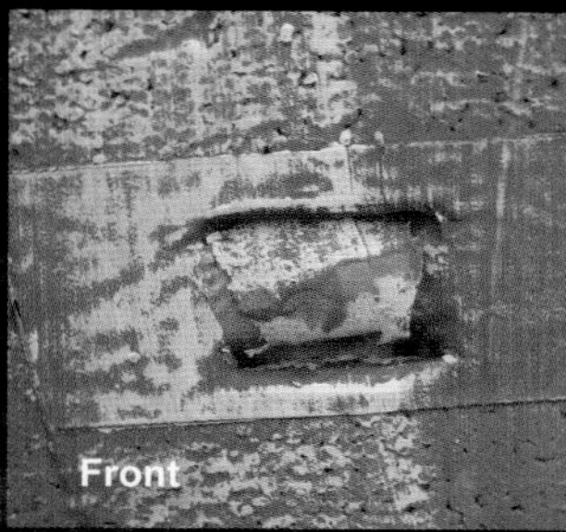

Front

Unassembled Styrofoam Parts

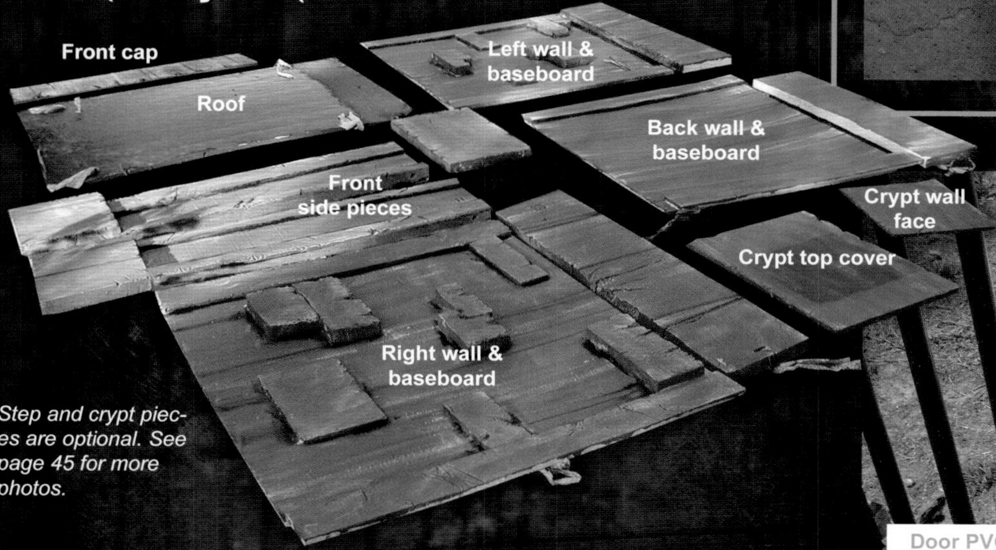

Front cap

Roof

Left wall & baseboard

Front side pieces

Back wall & baseboard

Crypt wall face

Crypt top cover

Right wall & baseboard

Step and crypt pieces are optional. See page 45 for more photos.

Door hinges

Door PVC bars

1' side panel width

1' side panel width

Insert fabric ties in Styrofoam anywhere close to a wooden support area. They will all tie on the inside of the structure.

Left and right front side walls

Side supports

Wall base attached before adding side wall

1'4" side panel base width

1'4" side panel base width

Creature Cages

Make your own creatures for the ultimate custom scare!

YOU WILL NEED: cages of various sizes, colors, and shapes; any sort of store-bought or handmade creatures to put in the cages; moss, straw, torn paper, pine straw, or leaves can be added for cage bedding. *Optionally,* add faux bones, body parts, or creature remains to the cages.

2

3

1

H anging from rafters, doorways, or dark corners of a room, cages filled with all manner of creatures make the perfect home-haunt decor. Combine different sizes and shapes of cages for a creepier look. Add moss, straw, or faux leaves from a garden center or hobby store to cover the bottom of the cages, and spray or hot-glue some webs around the outside for a haunting, unkempt look.

1 A pair of small, white owl statuettes look out from a nest of straw and spiderwebs.

Sometimes the inhabitants escape their confines!

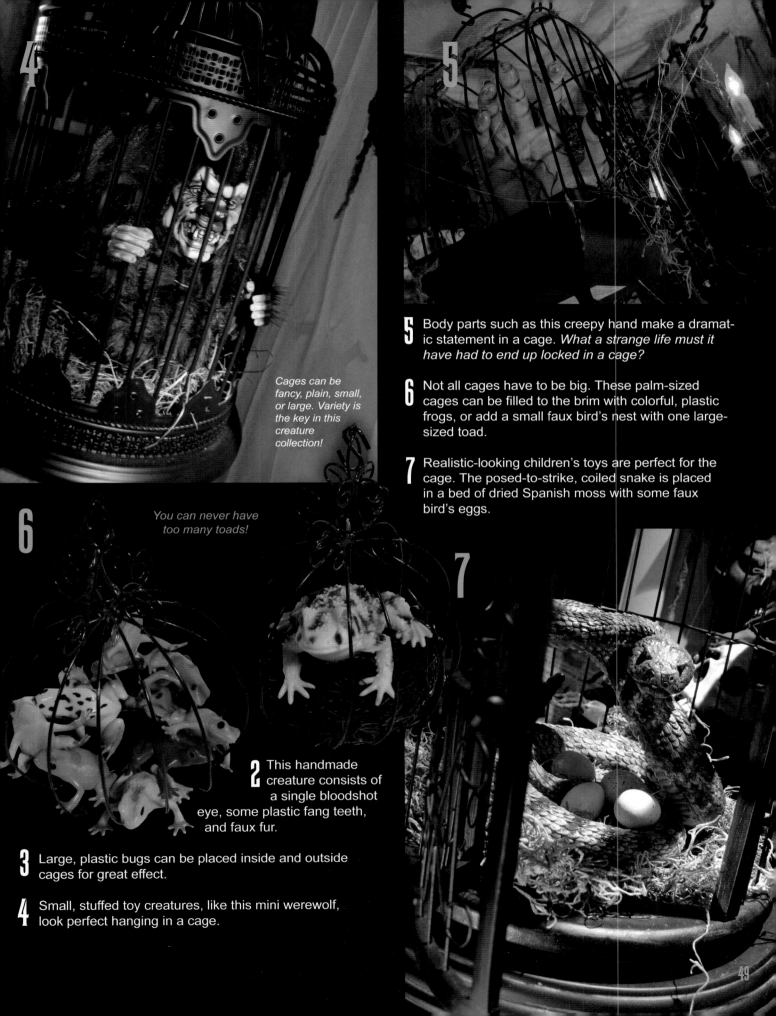

4

Cages can be fancy, plain, small, or large. Variety is the key in this creature collection!

5

5 Body parts such as this creepy hand make a dramatic statement in a cage. *What a strange life must it have had to end up locked in a cage?*

6 Not all cages have to be big. These palm-sized cages can be filled to the brim with colorful, plastic frogs, or add a small faux bird's nest with one large-sized toad.

7 Realistic-looking children's toys are perfect for the cage. The posed-to-strike, coiled snake is placed in a bed of dried Spanish moss with some faux bird's eggs.

6

You can never have too many toads!

7

2 This handmade creature consists of a single bloodshot eye, some plastic fang teeth, and faux fur.

3 Large, plastic bugs can be placed inside and outside cages for great effect.

4 Small, stuffed toy creatures, like this mini werewolf, look perfect hanging in a cage.

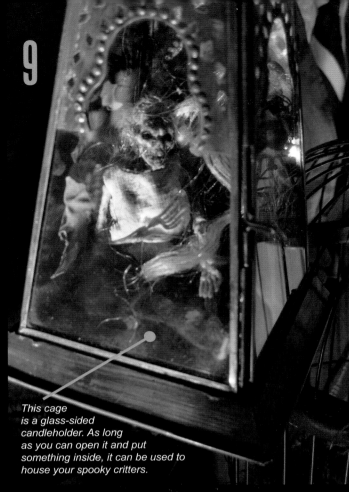

This cage is a glass-sided candleholder. As long as you can open it and put something inside, it can be used to house your spooky critters.

Think outside the *cage* for what occupants could go inside them. How about stone birds? The viewer may wonder if they could *come to life at any moment . . .*

Some caged beings may not have been well tended. This poor creature seems to have perished long ago, leaving its skeletal remains.

What devilish spell was cast upon this mummy's head? Add hot-glue spiderwebs for aged look.

Realistic mouse in a nest of straw. Add old tags or labels to cages for mad-lab appearance.

Animated children's toys such as this baby dinosaur, which makes sounds, spits a venomous stream of water, and snaps at unwary fingers, are perfect for creature cages. Here, some faux fern leaves and moss-covered branches were added to the cage for a homier look. Don't forget a few severed fingers or bones as a warning to guests to keep their fingers *out of reach!*

Haunt Tips

Cages can be placed on tables or suspended from chains of various heights.

Drape a cage with dark cloth or spiderweb cheesecloth to partially conceal what's inside.

Battery-operated candles placed inside cages create a spooky ambiance.

Hang a group of creature cages close together, then spray with a hot-glue spider webbing for an aged effect (see Spooky Chandelier in *Best of How to Haunt Your House, Volume I* for more details). Draping some spiderweb cheesecloth would also work well.

Severed prop finger

Grave Ghosts

YOU WILL NEED: 1" and 2" cell chicken wire by the roll, 24" wide, available at most hardware stores; wire cutters; lots of semitransparent fabric *(old curtains are perfect);* 3 or more yards of white cheesecloth; "S" hook painted black *(one for each hanging ghost);* scissors; thin wire *(or save the wire that wraps the chicken wire rolls);* mannequin head or small head-sized ball; one wire hanger; and protective gloves.
Optional: white netting fabric, which will glow in black light

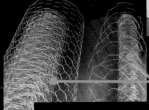

24" x 24" panel of 1" cell wire

1 Cut 24" length of chicken wire

Chicken wire sold in 1" or 2" cell sizes

Wear protective gloves when working with wire. Ends are **SHARP!**

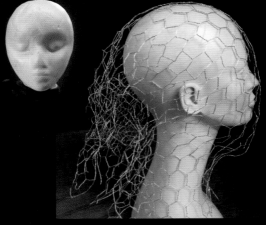

2 Bend chicken wire over the head form. The exact shape is not needed.

3 Bend the excess wire toward the back. Form a rough neck shape.

4 Remove head form and reshape wire as needed. Set wire head aside for later.

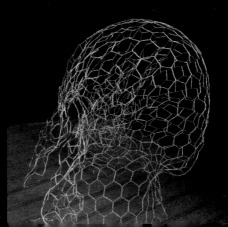

The Gray Lady, the Lady in Blue, the transparent silhouette on the widow's walk . . . we've all heard tales of those who refuse to leave this earthly realm. They wait and watch. They wander endlessly though the graveyard haze, unaware of the frightened gazes of the living who have glimpsed their unearthly forms. Lightweight ghosts make great props for Halloween or the home-haunt cemetery. Freestanding figures or half figures can be easily built with just a few simple materials.

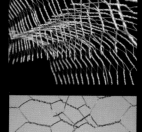

5 Overlap ends and twist when creating cylinder form seams.

6 Create 40" panel of 1" cell wire for torso cylinder.

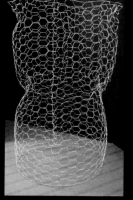

7 "Pinch" cells to form waist and shoulder points.

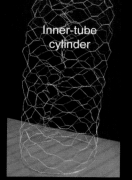

Inner-tube cylinder

8 Create second slightly smaller 2" cell torso cylinder.

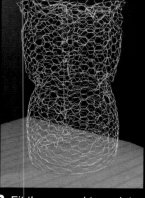

∨ Attach head

9 Fit the second torso into the first to add extra support.

Tube cylinder

24" height

Form two cylinders for arms.

10 Cut 32" length of 1" cell wire. Cut in half lengthways.

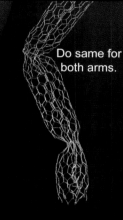

Do same for both arms.

11 Pinch at elbow and wrist joints, as shown.

12 Twist small wire at elbow joint to hold bent position.

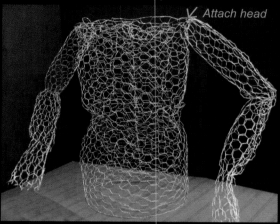

13 Use small wires to attach both arms to torso. Twist wire ends of head base to top of figure and shoulder area.

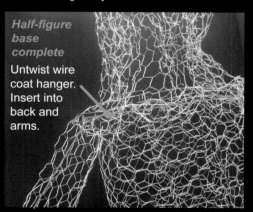

Half-figure base complete

Untwist wire coat hanger. Insert into back and arms.

14 Use small wires to attach head form to top of torso. Insert wire clothes hanger into back and into arms for support. Stop here for half-figure wire base.

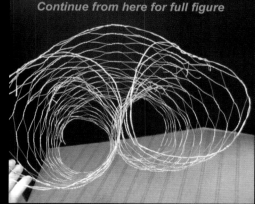

Continue from here for full figure

15 Roll 4' length of 2" cell wire into shape, as shown. Twist cell ends to back to hold shape. Make two.

16 Wrap 42" panel of 1" cell wire around the two pieces made. Twist ends at seam to hold.

---

17 Create tube with 1" cell wire. Cut in half. Place finished edges down.

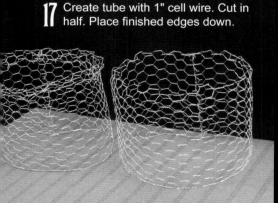

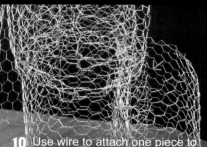

18 Use wire to attach one piece to bottom of torso and the second to the backside, slightly squished.

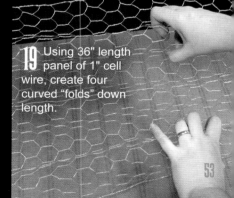

19 Using 36" length panel of 1" cell wire, create four curved "folds" down length.

53

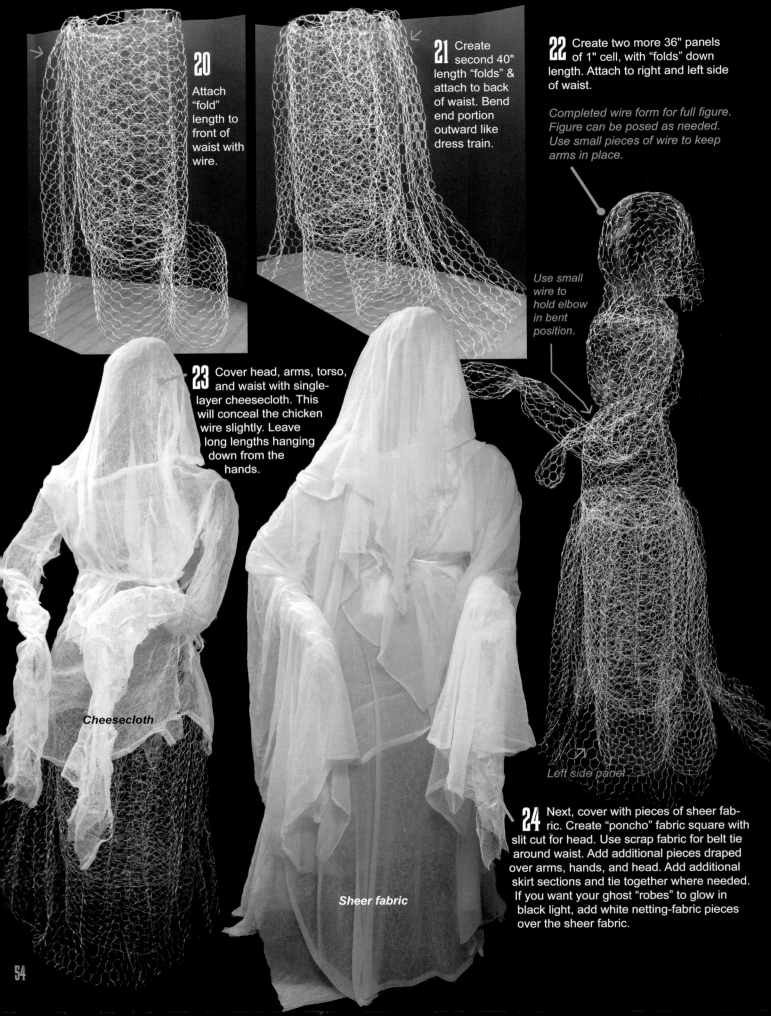

20 Attach "fold" length to front of waist with wire.

21 Create second 40" length "folds" & attach to back of waist. Bend end portion outward like dress train.

22 Create two more 36" panels of 1" cell, with "folds" down length. Attach to right and left side of waist.

Completed wire form for full figure. Figure can be posed as needed. Use small pieces of wire to keep arms in place.

Use small wire to hold elbow in bent position.

23 Cover head, arms, torso, and waist with single-layer cheesecloth. This will conceal the chicken wire slightly. Leave long lengths hanging down from the hands.

Cheesecloth

Sheer fabric

Left side panel

24 Next, cover with pieces of sheer fabric. Create "poncho" fabric square with slit cut for head. Use scrap fabric for belt tie around waist. Add additional pieces draped over arms, hands, and head. Add additional skirt sections and tie together where needed. If you want your ghost "robes" to glow in black light, add white netting-fabric pieces over the sheer fabric.

Half figure

Half figures are light enough to be suspended with string or strong fishing line. Black garden planter stakes can also be used to hold the half figures up off the ground and appear to float at night, as shown here.

The half and full figures can appear semitransparent with the addition of lighting or be suspended for a floating-ghost effect.

25 Once all the fabric has been added, cut holes and long, tattered end pieces like figures shown.

Here a small lantern is attached to the arm with wire, and a battery-operated candle added.

Full figure

Full figures can be placed outdoors in your home-haunt setting. Being lightweight, they are easy to move to a new location as needed. Use additional stakes as needed to keep from being blown over.

Be sure not to place hot lights near the ghost's fabric body.

"Día de los Muertos

Day of the Dead Candy Dish

YOU WILL NEED: one Styrofoam skull, a full-sized black plastic dinner plate, hot-glue gun and sticks, 13/64" drill bit, drill, white craft paint, ruler, black permanent marker, pencil, a collection of Halloween candy and lollipops. Optional for hollow skulls: 2" thick Styrofoam piece that can be used to fill the space below the jaw, and a serrated knife.

S erve up this *Day of the Dead* candy dish at your next Halloween party and stir up some colorful spirit fun! Candy corn, sugar pumpkins, and seasonal treats are the perfect offering for your party guests. Add a collec-tion of creepy and colorful lollipops, and crown this skull King of Halloween! This very easy candy dish prop can be used year after year as a table centerpiece or filled with trick-or-treat selections by the front door.

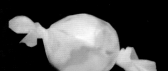

56

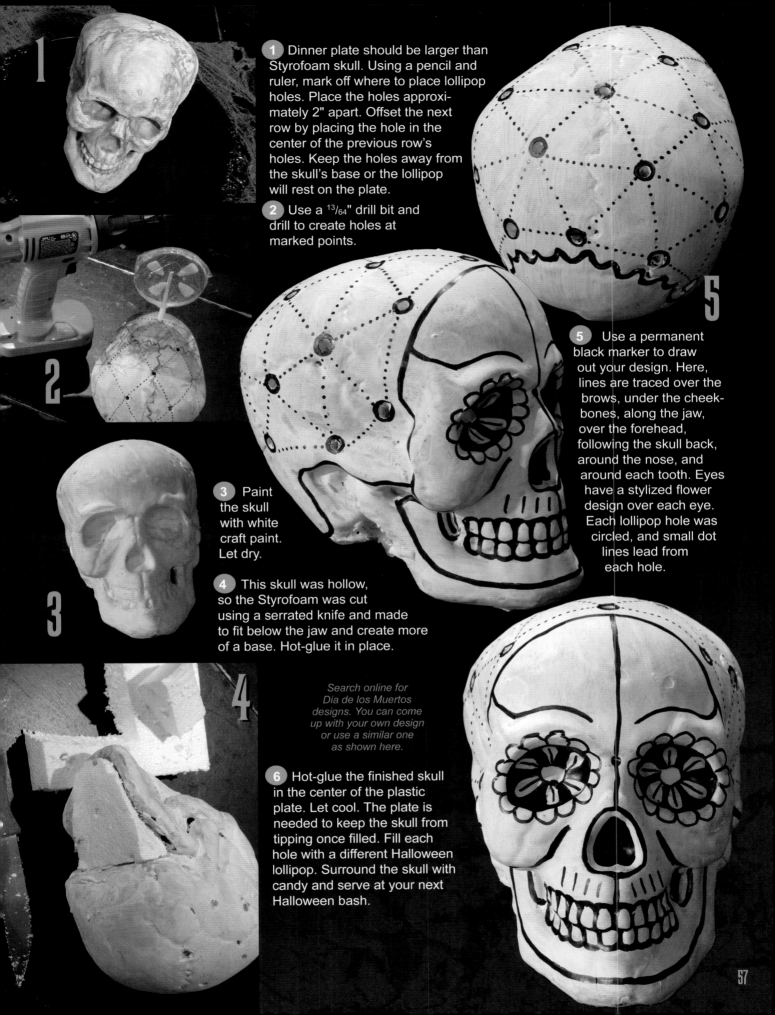

1 Dinner plate should be larger than Styrofoam skull. Using a pencil and ruler, mark off where to place lollipop holes. Place the holes approximately 2" apart. Offset the next row by placing the hole in the center of the previous row's holes. Keep the holes away from the skull's base or the lollipop will rest on the plate.

2 Use a $^{13}/_{64}$" drill bit and drill to create holes at marked points.

3 Paint the skull with white craft paint. Let dry.

4 This skull was hollow, so the Styrofoam was cut using a serrated knife and made to fit below the jaw and create more of a base. Hot-glue it in place.

Search online for Dia de los Muertos designs. You can come up with your own design or use a similar one as shown here.

5 Use a permanent black marker to draw out your design. Here, lines are traced over the brows, under the cheekbones, along the jaw, over the forehead, following the skull back, around the nose, and around each tooth. Eyes have a stylized flower design over each eye. Each lollipop hole was circled, and small dot lines lead from each hole.

6 Hot-glue the finished skull in the center of the plastic plate. Let cool. The plate is needed to keep the skull from tipping once filled. Fill each hole with a different Halloween lollipop. Surround the skull with candy and serve at your next Halloween bash.

Creepy Collections
The Bat Lantern

What makes a haunted house even creepier than the creepy collections of those who once inhabited the home? Taxidermy specimens, insect collections, and anything dark and decayed will do. Spend the year searching for your own unique and local bits and pieces. Then, create its very own special display box. Look up some Latin words and create some hand-drawn labels, using a quill pen and ink. When several of these dark obsessions are presented together, the creepy effect magnifies and draws visitors in for a closer inspection . . . giving you the perfect opportunity for a *good scare!*

YOU WILL NEED: one large-sized metal candle lantern with side door access, small battery-operated light, magnet, hot-glue gun and glue sticks, collection of faux plants, moss, sticks, two taxidermy bats (or bat props), latex gloves

Adding a light helps show off the interior occupants.

1 Hot-glue the magnet to the back of the battery-operated light. Let cool. Place the light somewhere in the top of the metal lantern. When on, it will illuminate the bats and foliage.

2 Create an arrangement of faux plants, moss, and sticks inside the lantern. If using taxidermy bats, use latex gloves to handle. Add a small amount of hot glue to attach bat feet to branch that will span top of lantern. Hot-glue or attach branch to inside top of lantern below light. Keep in mind you will still need to be able to access the light.

3 Shown below, a sample assortment of materials you can use to fill your bat habitat display.

Insect Display Case

YOU WILL NEED: thin Plexiglas *(old poster frame Plexiglas that has scratches works great!)*; utility knife; metal ruler; cutting board; wooden plaque *(found in craft stores)*; printed paper back sheet with insect designs and aged paper background; stained-glass foiling tape *(³⁄₁₆" copper color)*; hot-glue gun and glue sticks; craft glue; craft paints: brown, black, dark green, and light green; fan brush; tiny detail brush; scrapbook label frame; collection of insects *(your choice)*; wax; and picture hook

Unfinished wood plaque

1 Measure ½" along the plaque height and width. Determine height Plexiglas needs to be. Cut out Plexiglas pieces, using utility knife and metal ruler. Score and snap. Hot-glue inside edges of cut Plexiglas to connect five box sides. Cover outside edges with copper tape. Set aside. Paint wooden plaque with black craft paint. Let dry.

2 Print out back sheet with corresponding insect clip art and old paper background. Crumple the paper several times and then flatten out. Craft glue paper to plaque. Roll up edges for an edged look. Let dry.

3 Using a fan brush, carefully dab small amounts of brown paint along copper tape. Let dry. Do same using dark green. Let dry. Next, use light-green paint. Let dry. Use detail brush to apply thin black

line of paint along outside edges of copper tape *(resembles dirt)*. Wipe back toward tape with finger if too much is applied.

4 Use dabs of hot glue to apply insects to back sheet. Space the insects out in nice pattern.

5 Hot-glue the Plexiglas lid in place. Apply copper tape to Plexiglas and wood edge. Repeat *step 3*. Let dry. Rub a layer of wax over the black wood edges of plaque.

6 Glue a scrapbook label frame to one edge. Create a handwritten collection paper label. Insert into frame. Add picture hook to back of plaque.

Copper tape with aged patina effect using paint

Thin black line of paint applied to outside of copper tape

Label frame

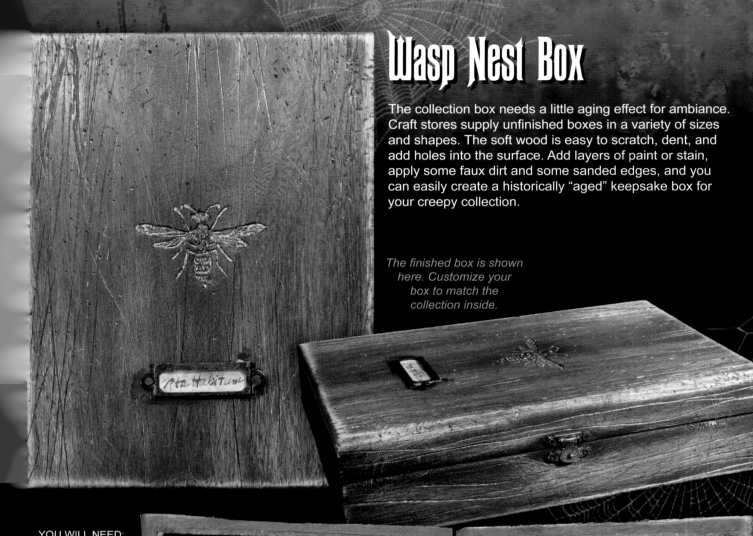

Wasp Nest Box

The collection box needs a little aging effect for ambiance. Craft stores supply unfinished boxes in a variety of sizes and shapes. The soft wood is easy to scratch, dent, and add holes into the surface. Add layers of paint or stain, apply some faux dirt and some sanded edges, and you can easily create a historically "aged" keepsake box for your creepy collection.

The finished box is shown here. Customize your box to match the collection inside.

YOU WILL NEED: unfinished wood hinged box *(found in craft stores)*; cork sheets; X-Acto knife; metal ruler; carbon paper; craft glue; straight pins; gold ink or paint; paintbrush; scrapbook label frame; paper label; sandpaper *(rough grit)*; quill pen; pen ink; assortment of tools for making scratches, dents, and small holes in wood; brown, red, and black craft paint; woodburning tool or Dremel tool; medium wood stain *(optional)*; brown tempera paint powder *(optional)*; wax *(clear car wax will work) (optional)*; hot-glue gun and sticks; and collected wasp nests *(or other creepy collection of your choice)*

1 Use an X-Acto knife and metal ruler to cut out pieces of cork to line inside of box and the box lid. Use craft glue to attach cork to wood. Let dry.

1

2 Gather an assortment of tools to make scratches, dents, cut marks, and holes on the outside of box. Follow the grain of the wood for scratches and cuts. More wear and tear would appear along box edges. Look for reference photos online in the form of antique boxes or furniture.

2

3 Find a clip art that has to do with the collection to go inside the box. Here a wasp image is used, since inside the box will be wasp nests. Choose an image that is appropriate. Use carbon paper and pencil to trace the image to your box top. You can use a woodburning tool or a Dremel tool with small tip *(or both, as shown here)* to trace out the pattern or carve the design into the box.

3

4 Use gold ink or gold paint to fill in the design.

4

5 Tint the box with either medium stain or water-based paints. Watered-down red craft paint was first applied here. Once dry, we mixed brown tempera powder with wax and rubbed it into the wood with a rag. Watered-down brown craft paint could also be used.

6 Use rough-grit sandpaper to remove color on edges and around clasp.

7 Use small amount of black craft paint to add back in some "dirt." Paint black edge where lid and box meet and down center of top of lid. Look at your reference materials for ideas on where to best add "dirt."

8 Add some more scratch and dent marks to edge areas. Sand some of the color, if needed. If too much of the gold was lost in the center design from the previous steps, add some back in.

9 Use quill pen and color inks to create handwritten labels to box. Scrapbook supplies include metal label frames of all sizes and shapes. These can also be further painted for aged look, as shown here. Glue label and frame to box. Let dry.

5

6

7

8

Aged label paper can be printed or hand-colored with tea dyes, paint, or careful burning of edges. Experiment with different processes.

9

PVC Candelabras

Let There Be Candlelight

YOU WILL NEED: various PVC 1" connection parts, 90-degree-angle PVC connections, four-way PVC connectors, 1" PVC pipe cut into desired lengths for each cande-labra; PVC glue, 1" width of fabric strips, cheesecloth, Monster Mud, black spray paint, PVC cutter tool, tall wax candles (or battery-operated candles)

You can never have too many candles for a spooky setting, but find-ing enough candelabras can be tricky. We came up with the easiest custom candleholders we could think of. They can hold one to five candles and have varied heights and widths.

1 Over the years, have amassed a collection of PVC connection parts choose from, bu could go to your home improvem store and find a ful of parts that a together with a 1 pipe. Choose wi parts for the bas each candlestick

2 Use PVC glue to a the parts for each dlestick. If making five-candle holder, will need to use PV glue to attach two 90-degree connect to the sides of the way connector.

3 Make a small batch of Monster Mud. Tear some fabric into 1" strips. Dip the fabric into the Mud. Wrap the mudded fabric around each candlestick, leaving the openings clear. For more-textural candles, wrap an outer layer of cheesecloth over the fabric. Let dry overnight.

5 Insert the candles, and the haunt props are ready to use.

4 Spray-paint the candlesticks black.

You could skip the fabric covering for a more industrial look.

Candles could also be painted, using the oxidizing paint for a metal look, or left white for a more ghostly appearance.

Flying Phantasms
The Dancing Bride & Groom

The spectral glow of the twilight lovers can be glimpsed hovering over the tombstones on All Hallows' Eve. Their silent dance is eternal, touching, and tragic. Having lost each other in life, they reunite *in death*.

YOU WILL NEED: any kind of plastics that are clear or white; plastic ties (*plastic cut into 2" strips*); craft wire; packing tape; packing plastic wrap; scissors; fishing line; large sewing needle; mannequin forms for male, female, or child; hot-glue gun and glue sticks; utility knife; plastic poly tubing on a roll for the air bag in sizes 2" and 3" wide; heat sealer *(Impulse Sealer);* gift shrink-wrap roll; small UV spotlights; blue-bulb shop light; heat gun; ceiling fan pole *(threaded on one end);* Styrofoam head form; white and black duct tape; plastic grocery bags; white spray paint; face masks; pipe cleaners; faux white roses; white netting fabric; any white decorative fabric or trim that is translucent; drinking straw; white wig *(for female);* white gloves *(male);* long white gloves *(female);* white child gloves; four-way metal pipe; screws; PVC pipe; PVC pipe cutters; four-way PVC connectors; PVC glue; translucent sheet plastic *(male hat);* Christmas tree turner

Packing-tape ghosts are fairly common online. We were trying to come up with a similar effect using less tape and more plastic that would stand up to the elements better and be able to support its own weight.

Mannequins

Groom Body

1 **Preparing the mannequins:** these mannequin forms are hollow with a front side only. To help fill out the shape, duct-tape the backside and attach at sides of mannequin, leaving an opening in the center back. Stuff the inside with plastic grocery bags (*or any other filling*).

2 Create a base to add wrap layers to. Using shrink-wrap, create a poncho with a hole for the neck area. Cover front and back of figure. Use packing tape to seal sides together.

3 With heat gun, gently shrink the plastic over the body form. This should not be smooth. Heat just enough to form basic body shape.

4 Wrap packing plastic around form, leaving ends of shoulders, neck, and legs open. Add approximately 4–6 layers.

MATERIALS: *1. heat sealer; 2. hot-glue gun; 3. heat gun; 4. glue sticks; 5. scissors; 6. utility knife; 7. clear tape; 8. shrink-wrap roll; 9. packing plastic roll; 10. roll of poly tubing plastic, 2" and 3" widths; 11. small packing plastic roll; 12. white netting fabric; 13. sealed poly tube heat sealed with air; 14. a drinking straw*

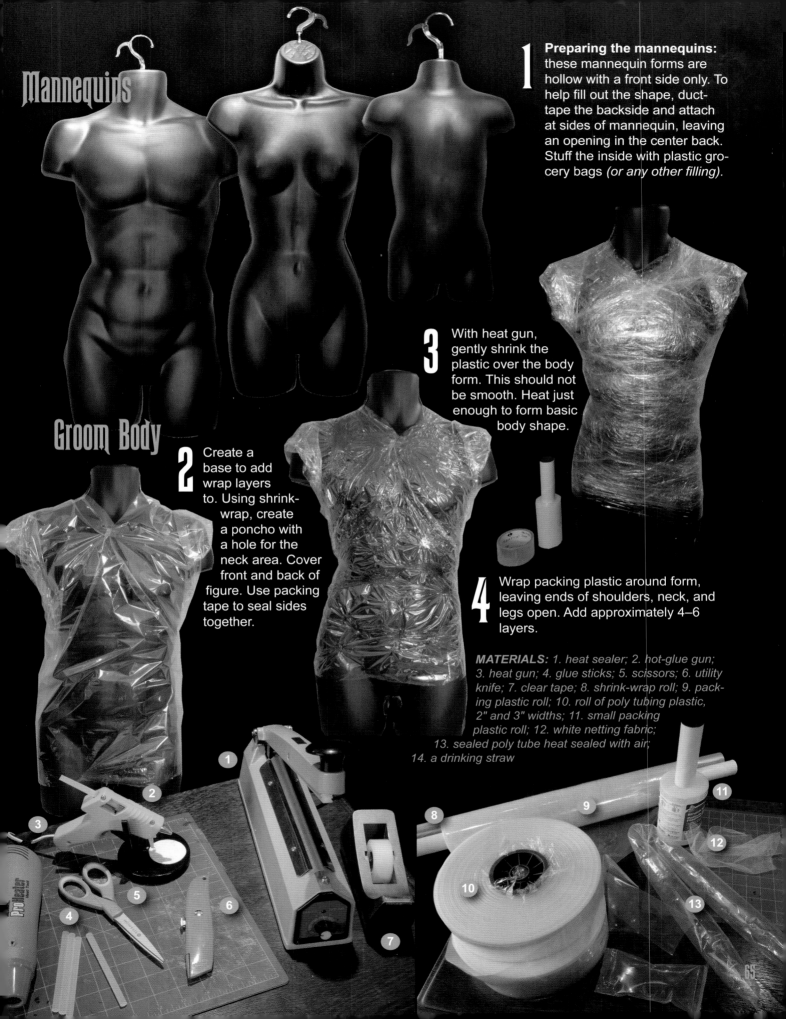

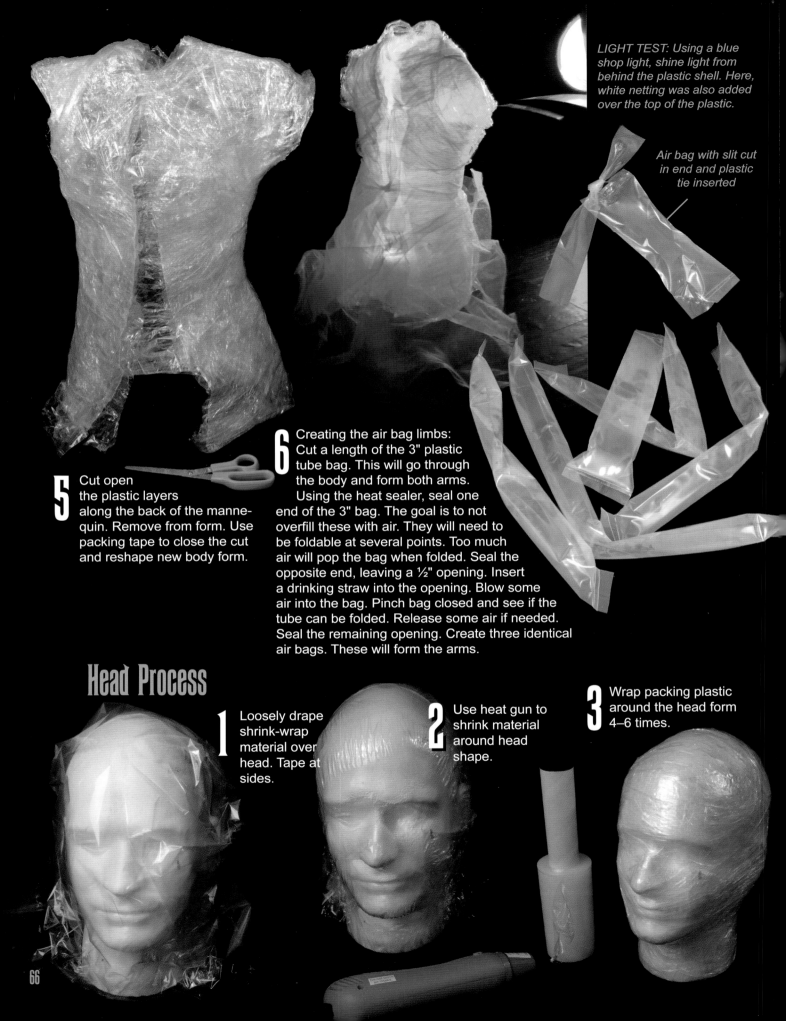

Air bag with slit cut in end and plastic tie inserted

5 Cut open the plastic layers along the back of the manne-quin. Remove from form. Use packing tape to close the cut and reshape new body form.

6 Creating the air bag limbs: Cut a length of the 3" plastic tube bag. This will go through the body and form both arms. Using the heat sealer, seal one end of the 3" bag. The goal is to not overfill these with air. They will need to be foldable at several points. Too much air will pop the bag when folded. Seal the opposite end, leaving a ½" opening. Insert a drinking straw into the opening. Blow some air into the bag. Pinch bag closed and see if the tube can be folded. Release some air if needed. Seal the remaining opening. Create three identical air bags. These will form the arms.

Head Process

1 Loosely drape shrink-wrap material over head. Tape at sides.

2 Use heat gun to shrink material around head shape.

3 Wrap packing plastic around the head form 4–6 times.

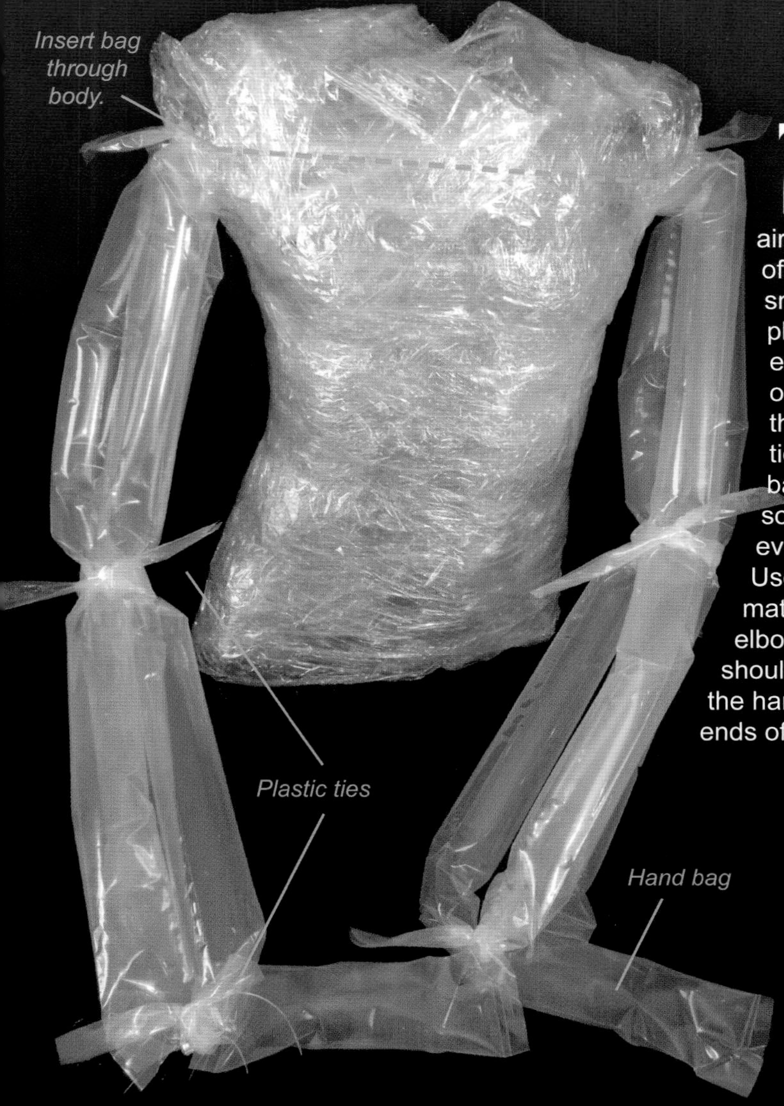

Insert bag through body.

7 Create two air bags the length of a hand. Cut a small slit in excess plastic at one end. Put a strip of plastic through this to create a tie. Insert the arm bags through body so the arms are even on both sides. Use strips of 2" poly material to tie off at elbows and shoulders. Tie on the hand bags to ends of arms.

Plastic ties

Hand bag

Groom Hat Process

1. Cut out hat pieces from thin, flat plastic sheet and tape together.
2. Wrap packing plastic around entire hat. Leave opening for head to fit into.

4 Cut a slit along back of head to remove from form.

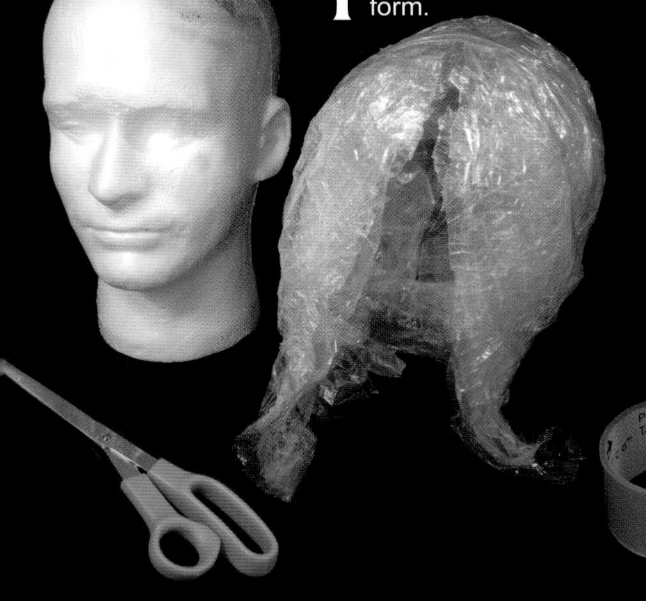

5 Use packing tape to close the back opening and reshape head.

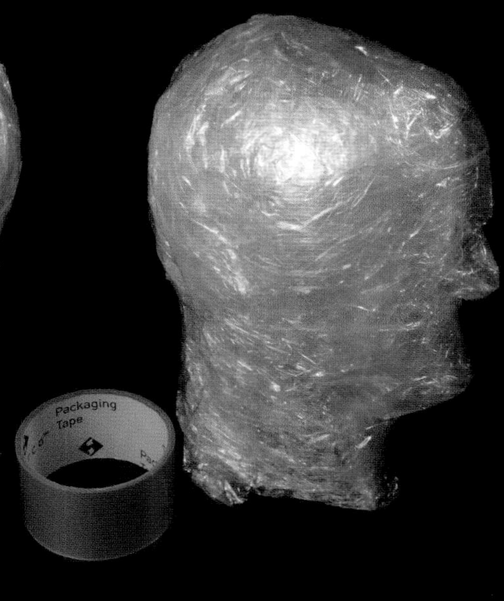

Packaging Tape

6 Insert several small air bags into head to hold shape.

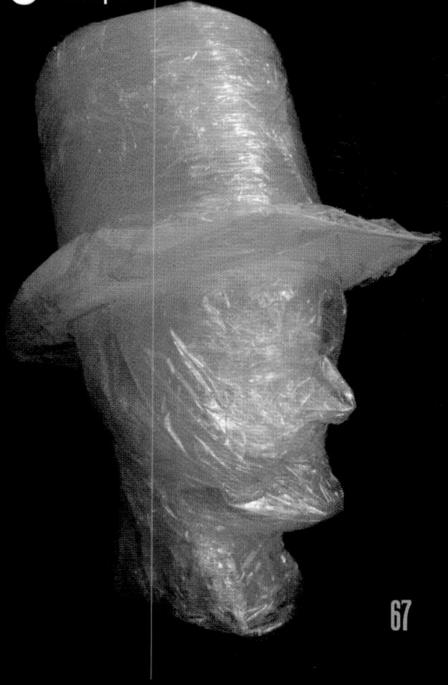

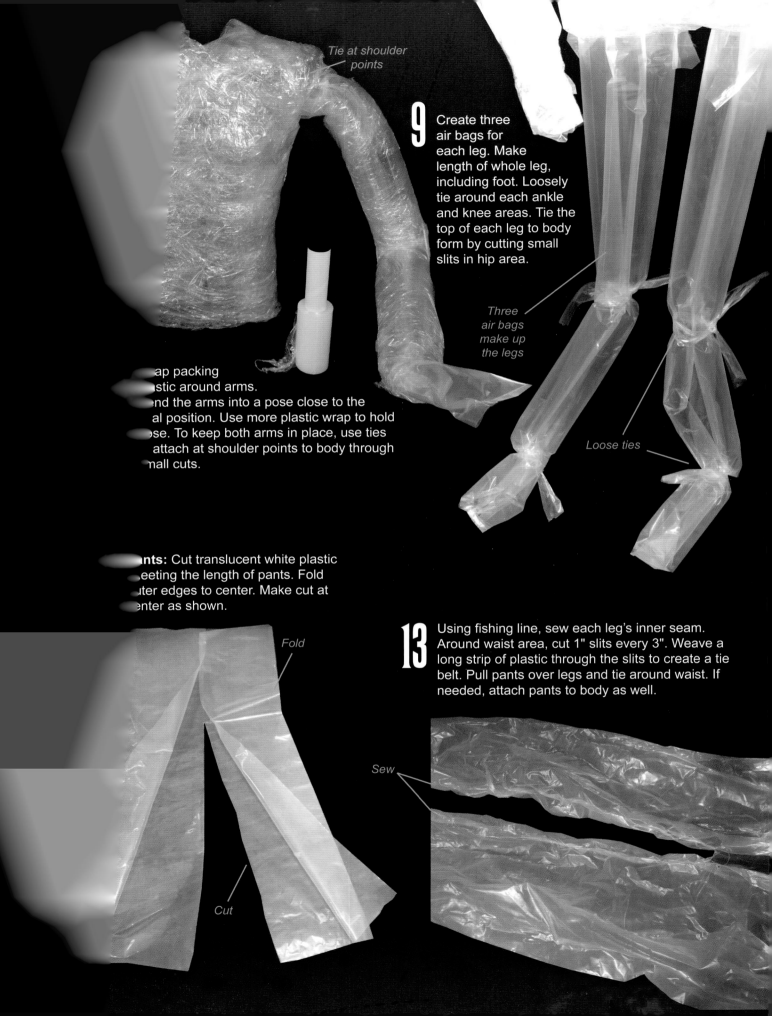

Tie at shoulder points

9 Create three air bags for each leg. Make length of whole leg, including foot. Loosely tie around each ankle and knee areas. Tie the top of each leg to body form by cutting small slits in hip area.

Three air bags make up the legs

Loose ties

...ap packing
...stic around arms.
...nd the arms into a pose close to the
...al position. Use more plastic wrap to hold
...se. To keep both arms in place, use ties
...attach at shoulder points to body through
...all cuts.

...nts: Cut translucent white plastic
...eeting the length of pants. Fold
...ter edges to center. Make cut at
...nter as shown.

Fold

13 Using fishing line, sew each leg's inner seam. Around waist area, cut 1" slits every 3". Weave a long strip of plastic through the slits to create a tie belt. Pull pants over legs and tie around waist. If needed, attach pants to body as well.

Sew

Cut

10

Bend each leg and foot into final pose and wrap in packing plastic.

11

Create air bag that is twice the length of the neck. Fold in half and insert in head. Wrap in packing plastic. Facemask is spray-painted white. Once dry, attach with mask elastic around head.

14

Sleeves: Cut length of plastic for each arm, leaving enough at end to fold up as a cuff. Sew along length, using same method as legs. Make a small slit at top of sleeve shoulder. Slide sleeve over each arm and attach to body with plastic tie.

Sew

Cuff

Fold

Body with sleeves and pants attached

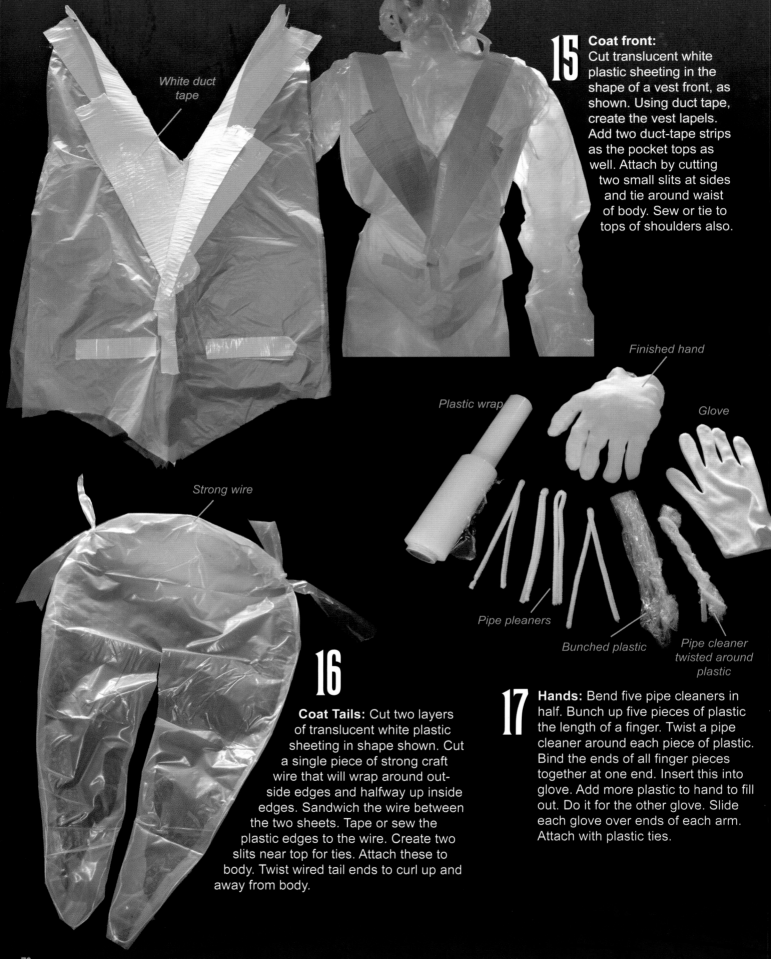

White duct tape

15 **Coat front:** Cut translucent white plastic sheeting in the shape of a vest front, as shown. Using duct tape, create the vest lapels. Add two duct-tape strips as the pocket tops as well. Attach by cutting two small slits at sides and tie around waist of body. Sew or tie to tops of shoulders also.

Finished hand

Plastic wrap

Glove

Strong wire

Pipe pleaners

Bunched plastic

Pipe cleaner twisted around plastic

16 **Coat Tails:** Cut two layers of translucent white plastic sheeting in shape shown. Cut a single piece of strong craft wire that will wrap around outside edges and halfway up inside edges. Sandwich the wire between the two sheets. Tape or sew the plastic edges to the wire. Create two slits near top for ties. Attach these to body. Twist wired tail ends to curl up and away from body.

17 **Hands:** Bend five pipe cleaners in half. Bunch up five pieces of plastic the length of a finger. Twist a pipe cleaner around each piece of plastic. Bind the ends of all finger pieces together at one end. Insert this into glove. Add more plastic to hand to fill out. Do it for the other glove. Slide each glove over ends of each arm. Attach with plastic ties.

18 **Coat cape:** Cut enough translucent white plastic to go around back and shoulders. Loosely gather top edge of cape, using fishing line. Cut a long rectangle for coat stand-up collar. Fold this in half and sew to cape along top edge. Cut a piece of distressed, white netting same size as cape. Sew this over plastic cape at base of collar.

White netting fabric overlay

Stand-up collar

Coat tail wire bent up on ends

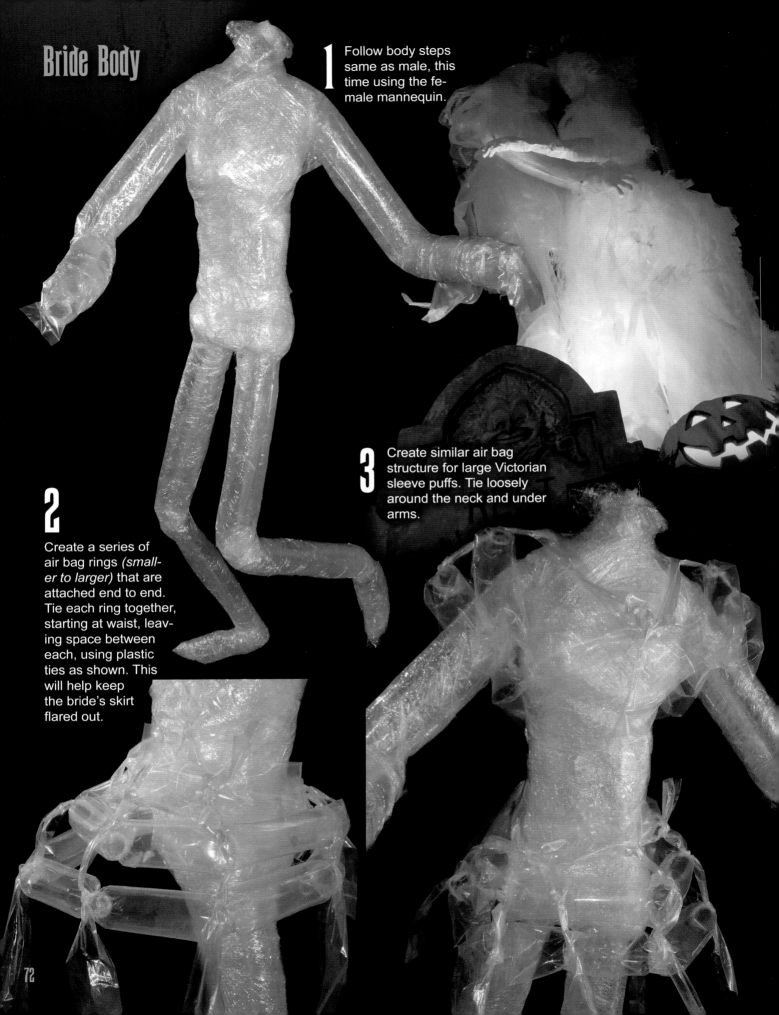

Bride Body

1 Follow body steps same as male, this time using the female mannequin.

2 Create a series of air bag rings *(smaller to larger)* that are attached end to end. Tie each ring together, starting at waist, leaving space between each, using plastic ties as shown. This will help keep the bride's skirt flared out.

3 Create similar air bag structure for large Victorian sleeve puffs. Tie loosely around the neck and under arms.

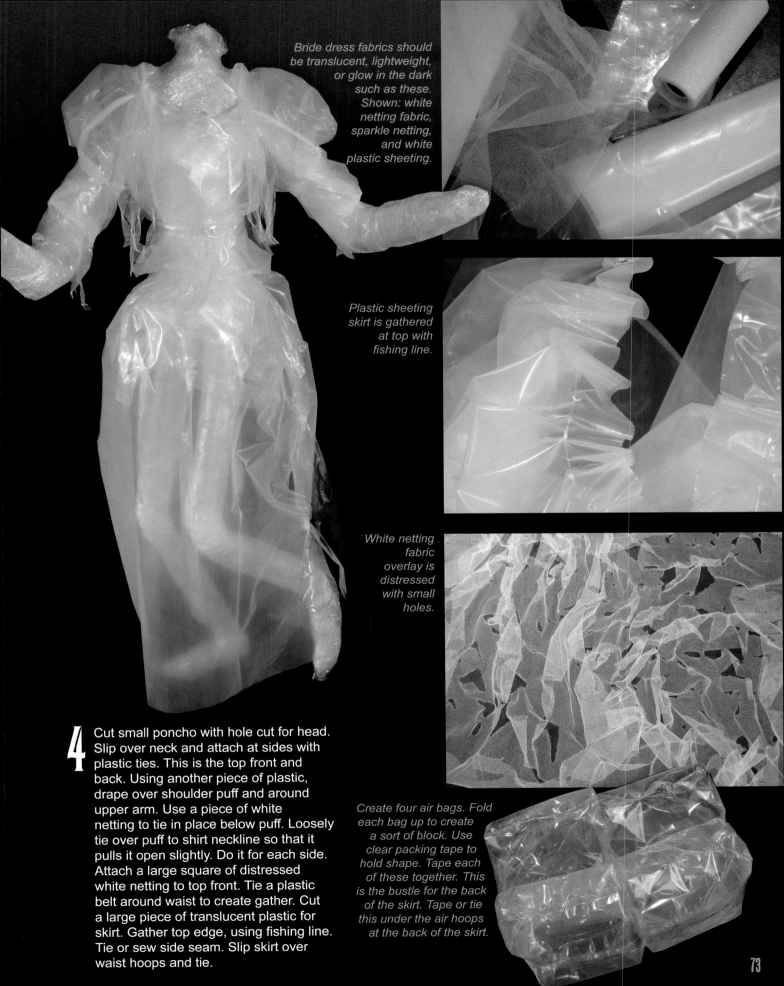

Bride dress fabrics should be translucent, lightweight, or glow in the dark such as these. Shown: white netting fabric, sparkle netting, and white plastic sheeting.

Plastic sheeting skirt is gathered at top with fishing line.

White netting fabric overlay is distressed with small holes.

4 Cut small poncho with hole cut for head. Slip over neck and attach at sides with plastic ties. This is the top front and back. Using another piece of plastic, drape over shoulder puff and around upper arm. Use a piece of white netting to tie in place below puff. Loosely tie over puff to shirt neckline so that it pulls it open slightly. Do it for each side. Attach a large square of distressed white netting to top front. Tie a plastic belt around waist to create gather. Cut a large piece of translucent plastic for skirt. Gather top edge, using fishing line. Tie or sew side seam. Slip skirt over waist hoops and tie.

Create four air bags. Fold each bag up to create a sort of block. Use clear packing tape to hold shape. Tape each of these together. This is the bustle for the back of the skirt. Tape or tie this under the air hoops at the back of the skirt.

5 **Bride head:** Create head like groom's. Add a female mask spray-painted white. Style a white wig for bride. Sew or tie wig to head. Create a ring of faux white roses and a distressed veil of white netting. Attach this to wig.

6 Create several pieces of distressed white netting. These will go over the skirt, top, and sleeves. The effect should be an old, moth-eaten wedding dress. Tie panels around body as needed. Add any other decorative accents for effect.

7 Create hands, using pipe cleaners same as groom. Add long, white gloves and slip over bride arms.

8 Cut ends of plastic sleeves and skirt as torn ends.

Completed bride ghost ready for her eternal dance

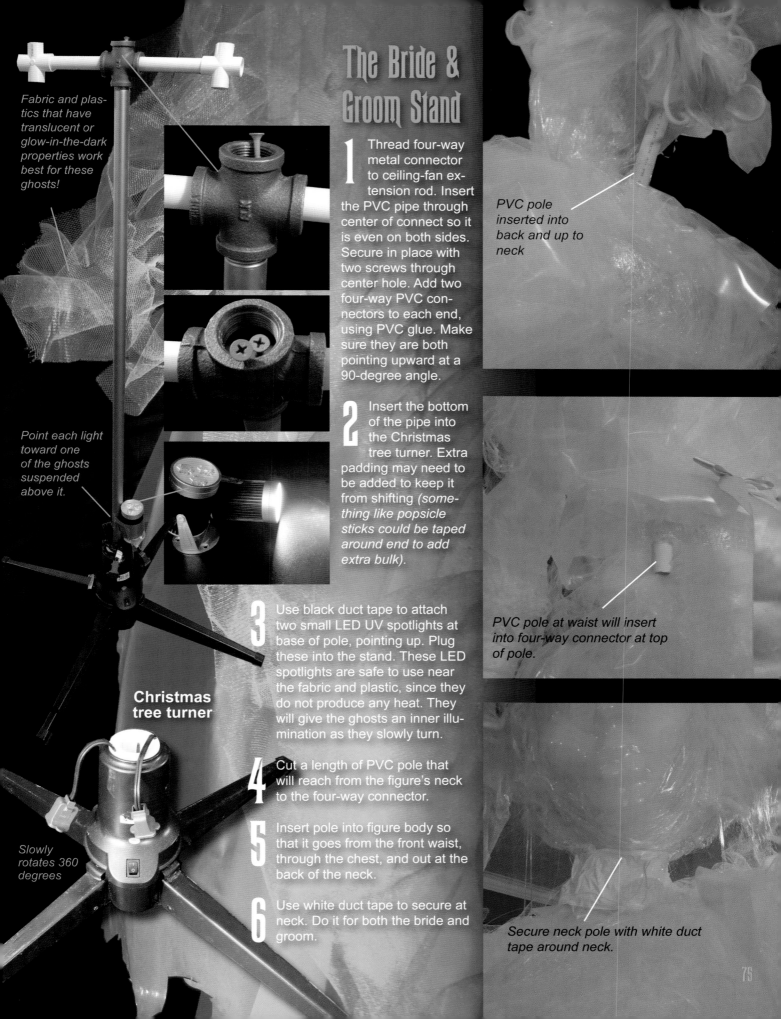

Fabric and plastics that have translucent or glow-in-the-dark properties work best for these ghosts!

Point each light toward one of the ghosts suspended above it.

Christmas tree turner

Slowly rotates 360 degrees

The Bride & Groom Stand

1 Thread four-way metal connector to ceiling-fan extension rod. Insert the PVC pipe through center of connect so it is even on both sides. Secure in place with two screws through center hole. Add two four-way PVC connectors to each end, using PVC glue. Make sure they are both pointing upward at a 90-degree angle.

2 Insert the bottom of the pipe into the Christmas tree turner. Extra padding may need to be added to keep it from shifting (something like popsicle sticks could be taped around end to add extra bulk).

3 Use black duct tape to attach two small LED UV spotlights at base of pole, pointing up. Plug these into the stand. These LED spotlights are safe to use near the fabric and plastic, since they do not produce any heat. They will give the ghosts an inner illumination as they slowly turn.

4 Cut a length of PVC pole that will reach from the figure's neck to the four-way connector.

5 Insert pole into figure body so that it goes from the front waist, through the chest, and out at the back of the neck.

6 Use white duct tape to secure at neck. Do it for both the bride and groom.

PVC pole inserted into back and up to neck

PVC pole at waist will insert into four-way connector at top of pole.

Secure neck pole with white duct tape around neck.

7 Insert body pole into four-way connectors, so the two figures face each other. DO NOT glue these poles to stand. You will want to be able to separate them when not on display.

8 Arrange figures' arms around each other, as though dancing. Pose fingers as needed. Use fishing line, if needed, to secure poses.

9 **Positioning props in graveyard:** Place heavy stones on Christmas tree turner arms. Hide external lights inside urns or other props and point up at figures. Black lights work well in this effect. Use tombstones to hide stand base and block view of lights.

The ghosts are semitransparent overall, with a few places that block more light. This helps drive the "ghost" effect of partially materialized.

10 *Turn on to test.* Figures should turn freely over tops of tombstones without getting caught on anything.

Ghosts glide over the walkway over the heads of guests.

White craft mask was added for the eerie face features.

The hands were simply the ends of the air bags wrapped in plastic wrap. Child's gloves could also be used.

Suspension poles seen during the day.

Child-Sized Ghosts

Smaller ghost versions can be made using the child form. Here, two ghost girls were used. Each was posed as if they were floating in the air. One girl wears a bonnet hat. The other has long curls and a large hair bow. Wrapping shrink-wrap around a cardboard tube made the curls. Heat the plastic curls up with a heat gun to set. Remove the cardboard and the curls hold their form.

In this effect, the Christmas tree turner rotated a black rod attached at the top, from which the ghosts were suspended on fishing line. The center pole was extended with a second pole to double its height. This was displayed near a walkway, so the ghost girls appeared to glide overhead. LED UV lights were pointed at each ghost, so they always had a light facing them as they turned.

The ghost clothing was made using thick, semiclear plastic and was gathered at the waist, arms, and neck as needed. Sew using fishing line or strips of plastic.

These lightweight ghosts could also be hung using fishing line just about anywhere. Hang in an upstairs window with a low light to be visible from the street. Hang at the top of a flight of stairs . . . or over a dining-room table. The possibilities are endless.

Beef-Netting Spiderwebs

Beef netting is a newer material being used by home-haunters. It is used to wrap meat in processing plants. The netting is purchased by the pound and comes on a roll in tube form. It must be first cut in half to create flat panels. Once cut, the length can be cut as needed. It weathers well and will get whiter after being in the sun a while. The edges, where cut, will also fray slightly, which looks good in the haunt setting! Beef-netting webs are also reusable and easy to store. Just bunch it up and store it in a container for next year.

To Cut a Beef-Netting Panel

1 Unroll a length of beef netting. Cut length needed. Cut tube in half to create panel.

2 Add two screws to the top of a doorframe or fence about 24" apart.

3 Place top edges of beef netting onto the screws. Pull material taut. If it's long enough, stand on the bottom edge.

4 Use a utility knife to cut as many holes as needed. *CAUTION!* Do not do this around kids or pets, and be careful cutting the holes!

To do both our front yard and backyard, we used a total of 70 pounds of beef-netting.

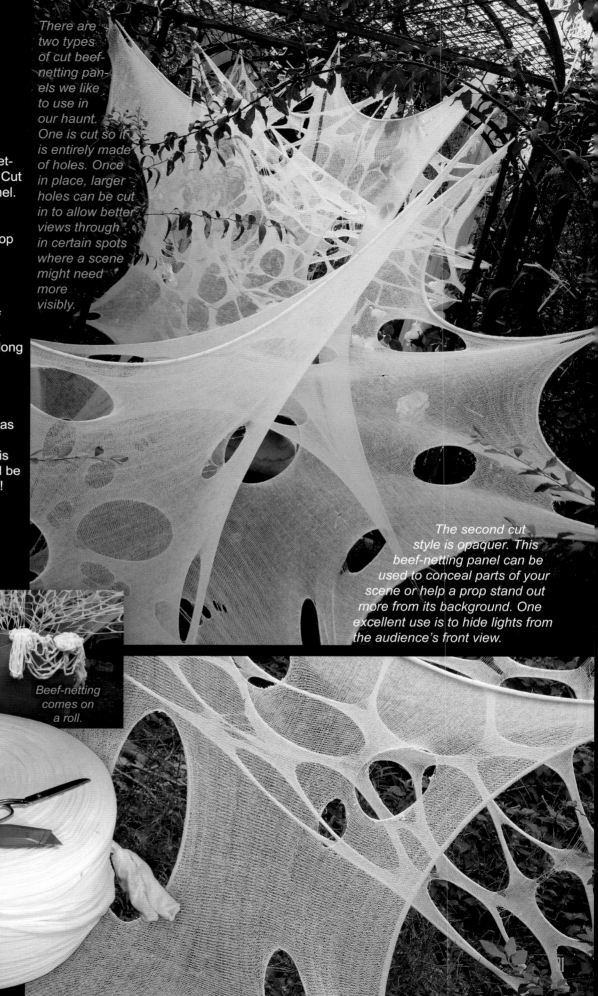

There are two types of cut beef-netting panels we like to use in our haunt. One is cut so it is entirely made of holes. Once in place, larger holes can be cut in to allow better views through in certain spots where a scene might need more visibly.

The second cut style is opaquer. This beef-netting panel can be used to conceal parts of your scene or help a prop stand out more from its background. One excellent use is to hide lights from the audience's front view.

Beef-netting comes on a roll.

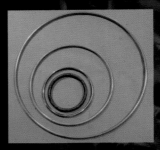

To create a large focal spiderweb or when hanging a HUGE web overhead, build a rope support structure first. Use a metal ring for the central web point. Any size of ring will do. Tie a rope to the ring and take it to the first connection and tie off. Then do it for the opposite side. Once the main lines are run, tie a few in-between ropes around the central ring, just as a real spider would do. Attach the beef-netting panels, each angling toward the central ring.

When hanging the beef-netting panels, layering is key. Pull a corner to the first connection point and tie off. Pull an opposite corner and tie off. If a corner doesn't reach, cut a thin 1" strip out of extra beef netting to use as a rope. Tie this to the end point on the panel, then to the connection point. Panels can be tied together to make wider sections. Beef netting can be dropped from rooflines, draped over trees, attached to bricks, or wrapped around captured victims. A little web imagination is all that is needed.

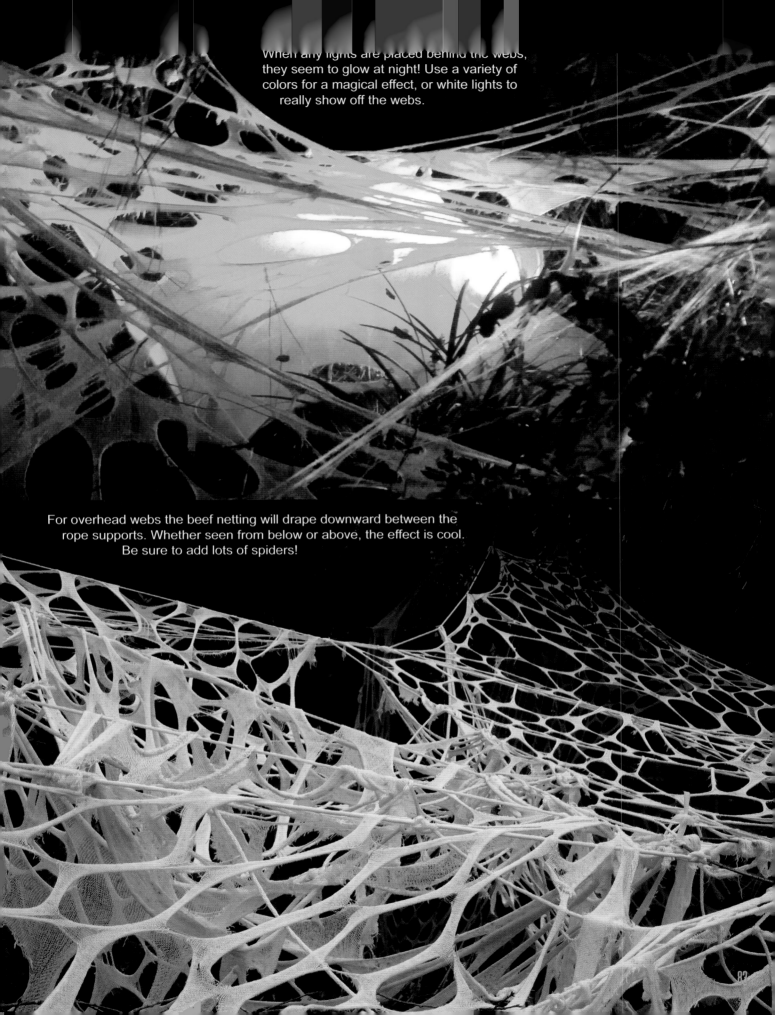

When any lights are placed behind the webs, they seem to glow at night! Use a variety of colors for a magical effect, or white lights to really show off the webs.

For overhead webs the beef netting will drape downward between the rope supports. Whether seen from below or above, the effect is cool. Be sure to add lots of spiders!

Web Victims

The Trick-or-Treaters Who Didn't Get Away!

They were big spiders with giant appetites! And the only thing they had on their minds was all those trick-or-treaters who so willingly wandered right into their web . . . *Everywhere one looked there were costumed bundles of web-wrapped treats.*

Body Form

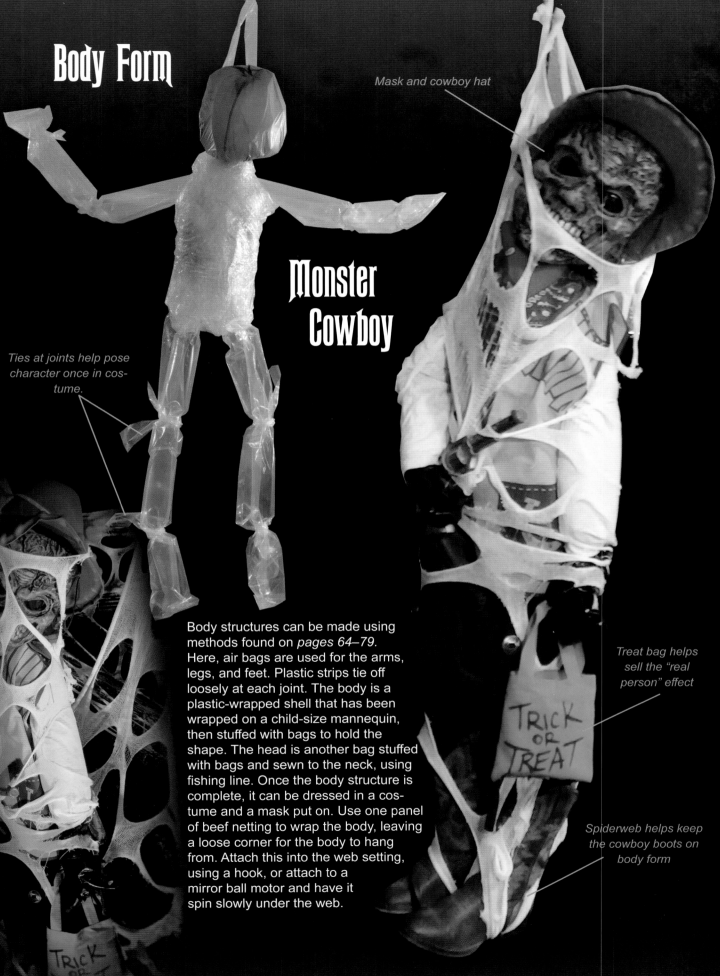

Mask and cowboy hat

Monster Cowboy

Ties at joints help pose character once in costume.

Body structures can be made using methods found on *pages 64–79*. Here, air bags are used for the arms, legs, and feet. Plastic strips tie off loosely at each joint. The body is a plastic-wrapped shell that has been wrapped on a child-size mannequin, then stuffed with bags to hold the shape. The head is another bag stuffed with bags and sewn to the neck, using fishing line. Once the body structure is complete, it can be dressed in a costume and a mask put on. Use one panel of beef netting to wrap the body, leaving a loose corner for the body to hang from. Attach this into the web setting, using a hook, or attach to a mirror ball motor and have it spin slowly under the web.

Treat bag helps sell the "real person" effect

Spiderweb helps keep the cowboy boots on body form

TRICK OR TREAT

An even quicker way to create a body is to use a child's one-piece sleep suit found at a secondhand store. It already has feet. Stuff the body with plastic bags and attach a mask for the head. Children's gloves can be used for hands. The fingers can be sewn into a pose or wires can be inserted to bend around the trick-or-treat bag.

Spider props

Creature

Flannel one-piece sleep clothes for kids are great for a quick body!

Robot

A robot costume was made using plastic cups, boxes, tin foil, hot glue, tape, and a pair of children's jeans.

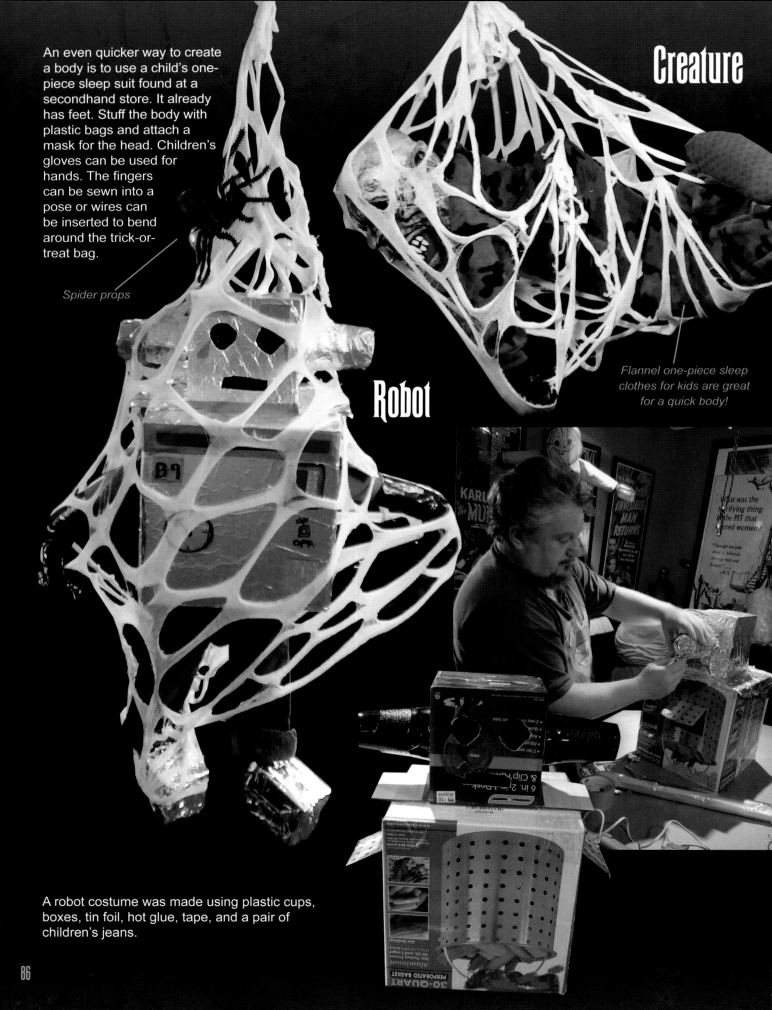

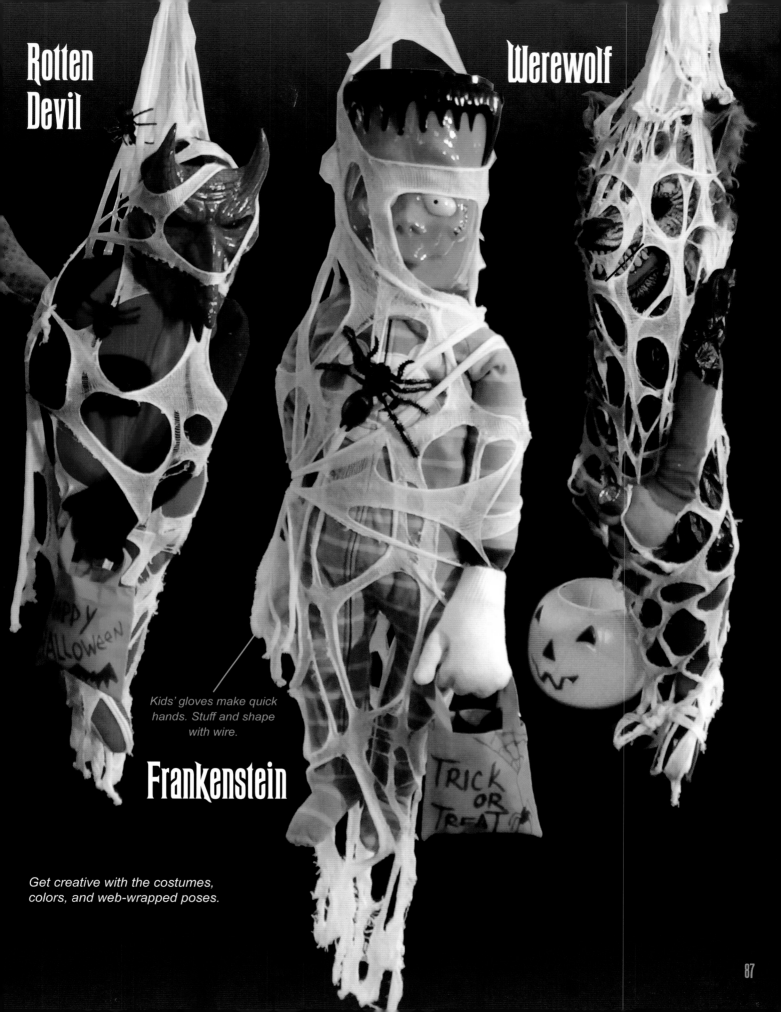

Rotten
Devil

Werewolf

Frankenstein

*Kids' gloves make quick
hands. Stuff and shape
with wire.*

HAPPY
HALLOWEEN

TRICK
OR
TREAT

*Get creative with the costumes,
colors, and web-wrapped poses.*

87

Jointed-Leg Spider

These giant webs are made by giant spiders!

YOU WILL NEED: several cans of expanding foam *(Great Stuff)*, 1½" PVC tubes cut into various sizes, eight PVC angle connectors, drill and ¼" drill bit, heat gun, clamps, ¼" hole washers, ¼" bolts, ¼" key nuts or ¼" lock nuts, wood for body base, twine rope, black spray paint, black duct tape, plastic blowup beach ball, hot-glue gun and sticks, plastic wrap *(Glad Press 'n Seal)*, tape, panty hose, clear plastic fillable Christmas ornaments *(for eyes)* or other lens-like eye parts, black and brown hairy yarns, small piece of plastic, needle and thread, wire, plastic bags *(or other stuffing)*

Nothing is creepier than spiders. Except, maybe, bigger spiders . . . *much, much-bigger spiders!* The kind that dine on pets, people, and trick-or-treaters!

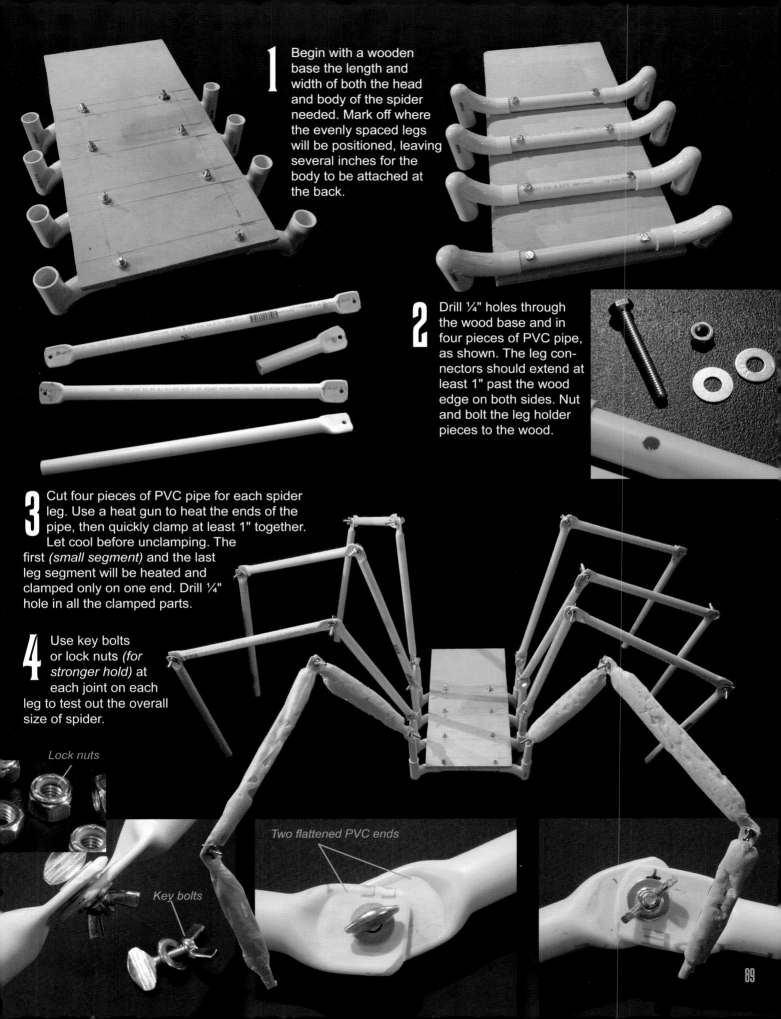

1 Begin with a wooden base the length and width of both the head and body of the spider needed. Mark off where the evenly spaced legs will be positioned, leaving several inches for the body to be attached at the back.

2 Drill ¼" holes through the wood base and in four pieces of PVC pipe, as shown. The leg connectors should extend at least 1" past the wood edge on both sides. Nut and bolt the leg holder pieces to the wood.

3 Cut four pieces of PVC pipe for each spider leg. Use a heat gun to heat the ends of the pipe, then quickly clamp at least 1" together. Let cool before unclamping. The first *(small segment)* and the last leg segment will be heated and clamped only on one end. Drill ¼" hole in all the clamped parts.

4 Use key bolts or lock nuts *(for stronger hold)* at each joint on each leg to test out the overall size of spider.

Lock nuts

Key bolts

Two flattened PVC ends

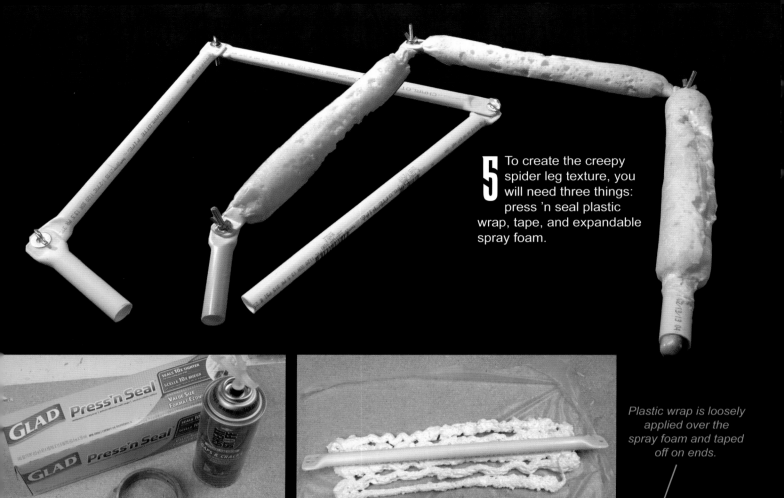

5 To create the creepy spider leg texture, you will need three things: press 'n seal plastic wrap, tape, and expandable spray foam.

Plastic wrap is loosely applied over the spray foam and taped off on ends.

6 Cut out a length of plastic wrap the length of one leg segment. Spray several rows of foam onto the plastic wrap. This should be shorter than the leg and not cover the leg ends. Place the leg segment on top of the foam. Carefully pull up the plastic wrap so it loosely surrounds the leg. There may be some gaps in the foam. This is OK. Tape the ends of the leg segment tightly so no foam will expand in these areas. Lean the package at an angle against a wall and let it set overnight.

7 Unwrap the leg segments. Peel off as much of the plastic as possible. If the leg bulk is not enough, you can do the process again over the dried foam or simply spray some onto the leg and let harden. We were going for a somewhat deteriorating, creepy look, so having some chunks missing was OK.

8 Once the leg segment size works, spray-paint the segments with black spray paint. Let dry.

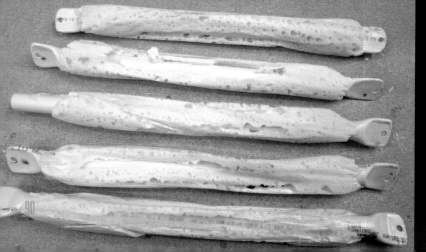

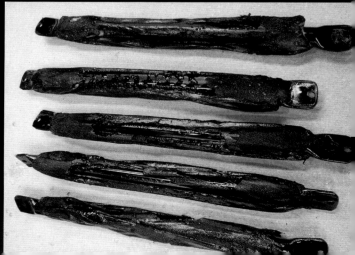

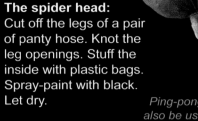

9 To form the spider body, blow up a beach ball that is the size of the spider body. Cover each side with spray foam. Be sure to leave a clear, uncovered area around the air-release valve on one end. Let harden and then cover the remaining sides. Once the foam has expanded and hardened, release the ball air and carefully remove the ball.

13 **The spider head:** Cut off the legs of a pair of panty hose. Knot the leg openings. Stuff the inside with plastic bags. Spray-paint with black. Let dry.

Ping-pong balls can also be used for eyes. Simply cut in half and spray-paint.

10 Spray-paint the spider body with black spray paint.

11 Trim the back end of the wooden base so it is curved as shown. Drill two ¼" holes just past the last leg segments in the base. Cut a piece of plastic that is slightly wider than the holes. Add matching holes in the plastic.

14 Open the plastic Christmas ornament holder into two parts. These will be the two larger spider eyes. For the two smaller eyes, we used children's toy spy scopes, but you can use anything you want, including smaller Christmas ornament holders. Spray-paint the inside of the eyes *(or outside, as needed)* in black and let dry.

15 Use "hairy" yarns in black and brown to over the spider's head.

12 Place the plastic inside the spider body, close to the opening. The plastic is used to keep the bolts from tearing through the spray foam body after being attached to the board. Spray-paint both sides of the wooden base and the leg connectors. Do not paint inside the leg connectors!

16 Hot-glue the eyes in place. Cover the head in the yarns, using hot glue. Careful not to touch the hot glue! Use a toothpick or stick to help lay down the yarn strands.

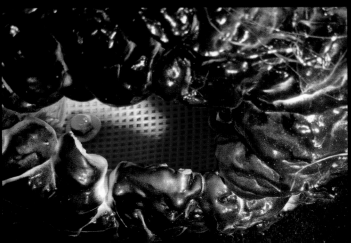

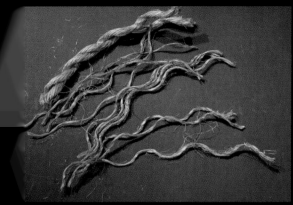

Alternate spider "hair" can be made from coco planter box liners, as in the filler spiders chapter.

17 **Spider fangs and pedipalp** *(two short leg parts next to fangs):* The fangs were created with bent wire, wrapped in plastic bag, covered in black duct tape, which taper at fang ends. Black "hairy" yarn is wrapped around the fangs toward back end to add some bulk. Two wire loops were left at center to be able to attach to wooden base. The pedipalp is created with PVC pipe that has been heated with heat gun and bent slightly. Cover with expanding foam and wipe down with stick to get smaller texture. Let harden. Spray-paint black. Wrap sparingly with hairy yarn that is hot-glued in place. Drill ¼" holes in the end and bolt to wooden base.

18 Cut a second pair of panty hose by removing the legs. Fit this over the wooden base, cutting holes for each of the leg connectors. Stuff a few plastic bags in to add bulk. Spray-paint black. Let dry.

19 Stitch head to this body pad at sides just to hold in place.

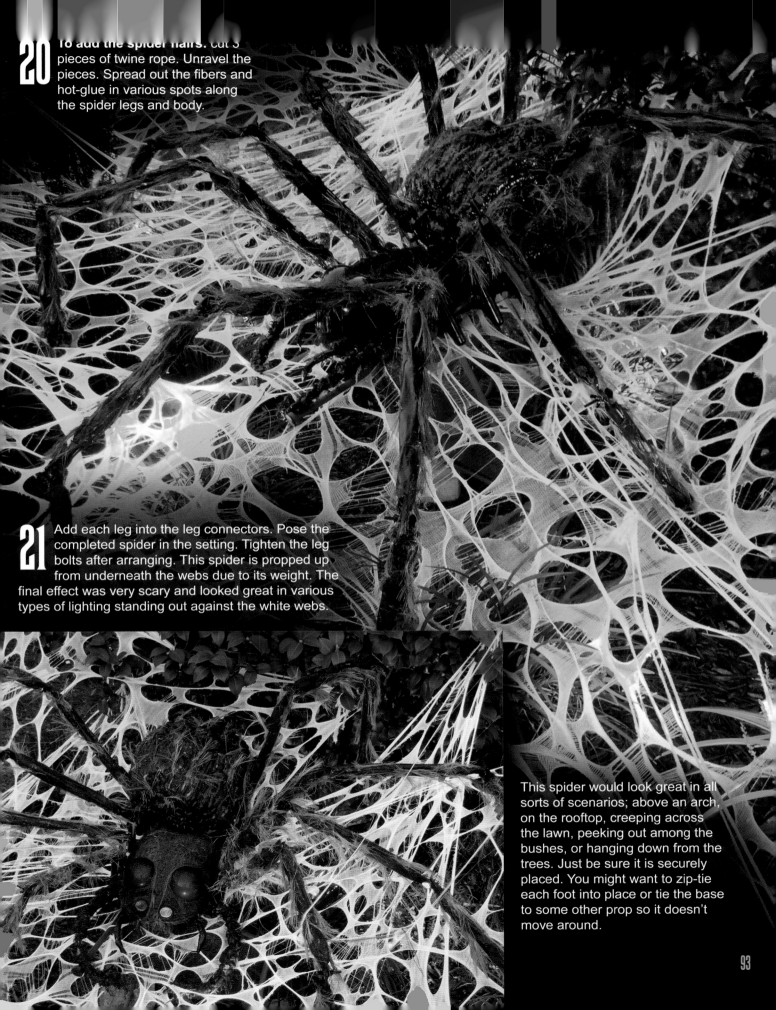

20 To add the spider hairs. cut 5 pieces of twine rope. Unravel the pieces. Spread out the fibers and hot-glue in various spots along the spider legs and body.

21 Add each leg into the leg connectors. Pose the completed spider in the setting. Tighten the leg bolts after arranging. This spider is propped up from underneath the webs due to its weight. The final effect was very scary and looked great in various types of lighting standing out against the white webs.

This spider would look great in all sorts of scenarios; above an arch, on the rooftop, creeping across the lawn, peeking out among the bushes, or hanging down from the trees. Just be sure it is securely placed. You might want to zip-tie each foot into place or tie the base to some other prop so it doesn't move around.

What Created the Giant Spiders?

Toxic Scene

YOU WILL NEED: 24" board to attach all parts, two wood blocks, windshield wiper motor, Monster Guts Pacemaker *(NOTE: Monster Guts Pacemaker has been replaced by PWM DC Motor Speed Controller)* OR Voltage Adapter to adjust speed of motor, two PVC legs, heat gun and clamps, small chain, key rings, screws, drill, washers and metal spacers, flat metal bars or flat metal bracket, adjustable double-sided eye hooks, small eye screws, C clamps, small bolts and nuts, ½" L brackets, spray foam, black spray paint, green and yellow florescent spray paint, spider leg "hair" *(rope or coco planter fibers)*, black trash cans, "toxic" labels, black duct tape, bubble maker, bubble juice, green shop light, utility knife, black zip-ties, bucket with lid, black flex hose, fog machine, PVC pipe with 90-degree angle to fit end of fog machine, drill, metal pins *(inserts into washers but still allows them to move)*, glue gun and glue sticks

Kicking-Spider-Legs Motor Project

This project is based on the kicking-legs motor projects found online in the home-haunt community. Instead of two human legs kicking, we turned the PVC "legs" upside down and made them into two spider legs sticking out of a toxic barrel! We also used Monster Guts Pacemaker in order to slow down the speed of the windshield wiper motor.

NOTE: Monster Guts Pacemaker has been replaced by PWM DC Motor Speed Controller.

94

1 The baseboard is lifted on the front end with a wooden block. A second wooden block is used to level off the metal bars' rotation point, so it is level with the motor arm. Chains connected to both ends of the second metal bar are then connected to each leg, lifting it in turn.

2 Each leg chain is connected to a key ring and a double-sided adjustable eye hook. These are then connected to another key ring and a small eye hook screwed into the top-facing surface of each leg. Some experimenting is required to figure out how much length is needed to reach each leg. Use the adjustable eye hook to shorten or lengthen the amount.

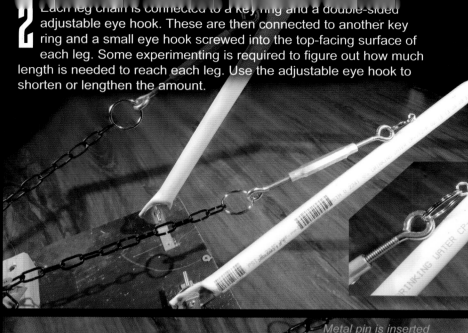

3 On the first metal bar, drill approximately ⅜" holes in each end. The first hole connects with the motor arm. For the second hole, use washers on top and bottom and through the end hole of the second metal bar and connect all, using a pin. Attach chain ends to the second metal plate at each side.

Metal pin is inserted through washers but still allows it to rotate.

Metal spacers

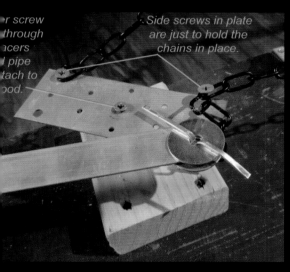

r screw through acers l pipe tach to ood.

Side screws in plate are just to hold the chains in place.

4 A variety of spacers were used to make the metal bars level with the motor arm. A long screw runs from the center of the second metal plate and into the wood block. It should rotate freely.

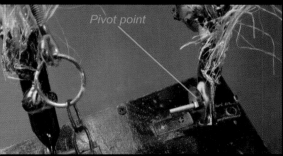

Pivot point

6 Motor is held to wood base by using C clamps and screws. First metal bar hole is placed over motor arm nut. If adjustments are needed *(as shown here)*, drill more holes in metal end until the right placement is achieved.

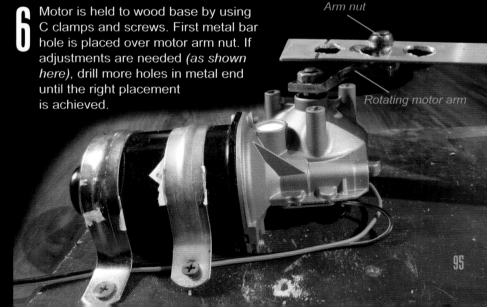

Arm nut

Rotating motor arm

5 Each PVC leg is flattened on one end, using a heat gun and clamps. Drill a ¼" hole in center of each flattened part. Screw L brackets on either side of legs, with a little space in between. Place the washers on each side of flattened parts. Use a bolt and nut to hold in place. Legs should be able to pivot easily.

7 Spray-foam each leg, careful not to cover the ends or eye hooks. Let dry.

8 Two more static spider legs can be placed on either side of the base-board for effect.

Static Leg

Motorized legs

9 Once spray foam is set, spray-paint black. Let dry. Hot-glue either rope hair or planter liner hair down the length of each leg.

Static leg

Toxic Barrel Bubbler

Toxic barrels are made from large black trash cans. Spray-foam around top in several passes. Let dry. Then spray-paint green and yellow fluorescent paints. Let dry. Add variety of toxic stickers to can sides. For toxic barrels that are standing upright, place a bubble maker such as this one inside with a light.

For the spider leg kicker, the toxic spray foam was made in two parts to help conceal the inner workings of the spider legs and allow for adjustments. Zip-tie a green light above the kicker to the top of the trash can.

Cut two holes in back end of trash can. One hole is to run any electrical cords out. The second to attach the black flex hose for the fog machine. Use black duct tape to seal flex tube to trash can.

The fog added to the eerie scene!

Inside of the spider leg kicker garbage can:
light is zip-tied to top in back

Testing the fog
during the day

Ice surrounding PVC pipe

Ice in the chiller box cools the fog down and allows it to stay closer to the ground.

Toxic barrel bubbler

Small chiller box with lid

Toxic barrel bubbler

Small chiller

PVC pipe from chiller to fog machine

Pacemaker / speed-controller device

Tube that sends chilled fog into leg kicker can

Fog machine

Toxic Barrel Fogger

Small bucket chiller with PVC pipe inserted into one side with 90-degree angle inside to release the fog inside the closed bucket. The ice chills the fog and lets it escape out the black flex tube and into the spider kicker toxic can. The effect at night was great!

Weathered Urns

Set the Table or the Family Plot

YOU WILL NEED: two sets of plastic bowls in various sizes; urn-base-shaped parts *(flowerpots, flower vases, small garbage can, etc.);* Gorilla Glue for plastic; scrap cloth; scrap Styrofoam; various faux flowers and leaves; Monster Mud; white, gray, and black craft paint; sponge; brush; toothbrush; hot-glue gun and sticks; duct tape

S et the table or the family plot with these weathered urns. Time has aged them well, and they add just the right spooky flare to the chilly season. Go for either a hand-carved stone look or a rusty metal patina on a variety of shapes and sizes.

1 First, determine the overall shape for each urn. Try out various sizes and stacking order.

2 Apply Gorilla Glue to all plastic parts. Let dry overnight. Do not glue any cloth parts. Styrofoam can be used to roughly carve out some urn handles, if needed. Glue these in place and reinforce with duct tape to hold in place.

New or old planters make great urn bases.

Glue two matching-size bowls on top of each other.

Draped cloth is Monster-Mudded separately.

Faux flowers and leaves are hot-glued on.

3 Hot-glue faux flowers and leaves around various parts of urns. Make sure to add some decorative parts to the top.

Roses drooping down-ward are sadder.

Time for the kids to get muddy!

Be sure to cover all the crevices around the faux plant parts.

4 Use Monster Mud on the entire urn, including all flowers and leaves. If the urn has a fabric drape, dip the fabric into the Monster Mud and drape ends over urn handles. Let dry overnight.

5 Use a loose mix of white, gray, and black craft paint to cover the entire urn. Let dry.

6 Next, use a toothbrush to spray random dots in white and black over the surface. Let dry.

7 Last, tone down the paint effect by dabbing more of the mixture of white and gray craft paint over the top, using a crumpled plastic bag or rag. Do this sparingly, letting the previous layers show through. Let dry.

A weathered look comes from the lighter areas around the seams.

What spirits wander here in the deep, dark shadows of a forgotten cemetery?

Making an Entrance
Invasion of the Spiders!

When the Mitchells decide to do a '50s B-movie-inspired theme of giant spiders . . . they also have to do a massive amount of giant spiderwebs! That means *70+ pounds* of hand-cut spider webbing that must be hung, piece by piece, from the roof, the trees, the bushes, and every other thing or person who happened to be around the haunt.

BEWARE OF SPIDERS!

Beef-netting spider's web was used for most of the scene, but store-bought stretch webbing was also mixed in, going from the roof tops to the tallest bushes for a bit of fine detail.

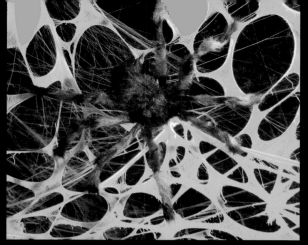

1 Entrance Hack

Don't forget the spiders—whether they are handmade or store-bought, they are the scary stars of the theme! But, on occasion, even spiders have a sense of humor! The spider on the right was spotted hanging out in a baby carriage with a baby bottle in its mouth and a bib that said, *"Dinner's on me."*

2 Entrance Hack

Go high and low with the decorations. Don't just make everything at eye level. Get your audience scared with things nervously high overhead or coming in low around their feet. They will literally be surrounded with scares! These spiderwebs reached up all the way to the rooftops and back down to the ground.

Spider catches the cat and takes him for a spin . . .

3 Entrance Hack

Use hidden mirror ball motors to slowly rotate small props in the setting. The left side photo has a motor hidden inside the spider's head. A spider's web dangles an upside-down cat!

4 Entrance Hack

Instead of using fencing to guide the trick-or-treaters where to go, use paths lined with the beef-netting spider's web. Tie the webs to furniture, trees, or props and use tent stakes to secure to the ground around the path.

BEWARE! OF SPIDERS!

The path from the entrance is treacherous. Careful . . . you may not make it out the other side!

5 Entrance Hack Use high-contrast silhouettes to your nighttime advantage. Light-colored webs with dark spider shapes are a great example. Your main props should be detailed, but ones farther away can be less detailed as long as the spooky silhouette still reads *scary*. It still sells the story, and the audience will get it!

The Mitchells' costumes for a 1950s lady, and Acme bug sprayer complete with preattached spiders

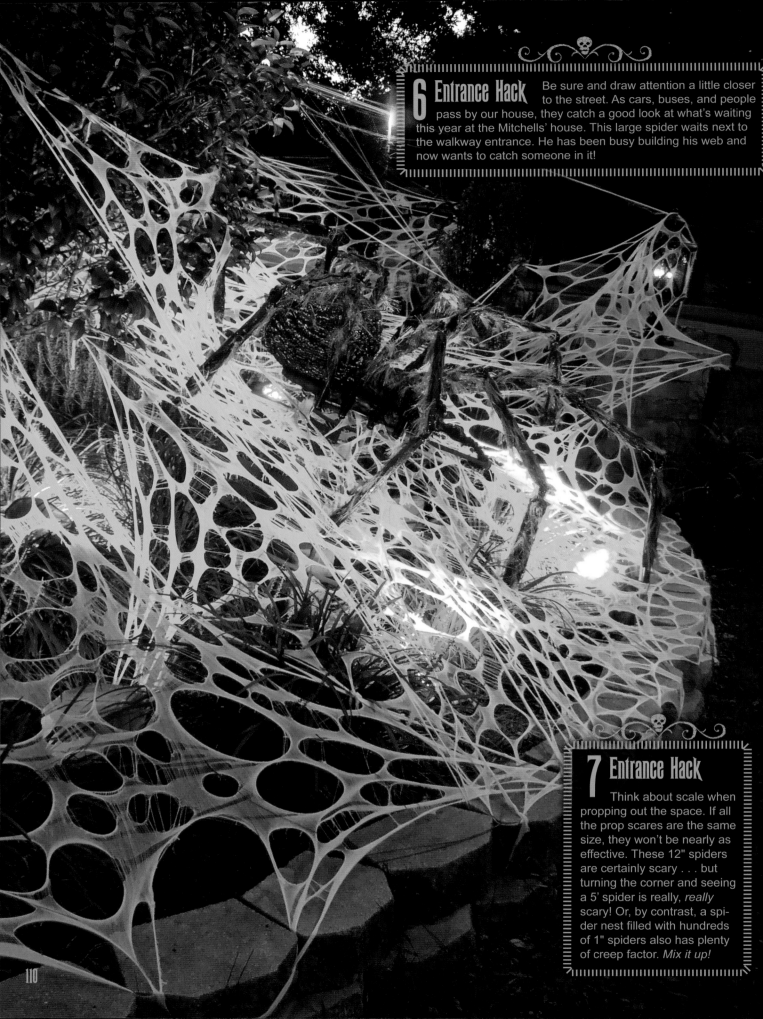

6 Entrance Hack Be sure and draw attention a little closer to the street. As cars, buses, and people pass by our house, they catch a good look at what's waiting this year at the Mitchells' house. This large spider waits next to the walkway entrance. He has been busy building his web and now wants to catch someone in it!

7 Entrance Hack

Think about scale when propping out the space. If all the prop scares are the same size, they won't be nearly as effective. These 12" spiders are certainly scary . . . but turning the corner and seeing a 5' spider is really, *really* scary! Or, by contrast, a spider nest filled with hundreds of 1" spiders also has plenty of creep factor. *Mix it up!*

Sometimes even we run screaming from our own creations!

Spider's nest filled with hungry baby spiders!

Disco ball motor rotates web-holding figure.

This poor trick-or-treater dressed as Spider-Man has two spiders clinging to him as he spins, using a disco ball motor. To add to the effect, add a flashlight that is turned on in one hand, and a trick-or-treat bucket in the other hand.

An unlucky trick-or-treater who didn't make it out of the web!

Setting the Stage:
Inside the Haunted House
through the Years

We love our fear of the unknown. We like mysterious cold spots and things that make us jump. We smile at being caught off guard and laugh often when something makes our hair stand on end. We are at home with ghosts and spooks and creaky doors. It's Halloween again—*our favorite time of the year.* Time to embrace our fear of the dark and things that go bump in the night.

2 Haunt Set Hack

Something every haunted house needs—*a skeleton or two.* Have them join the party by dressing them up in a fun costume. Add a wig and accessories and pose them at the table or in a chair. From deceased fortune-tellers to creepy characters, it's easy to add a layer of scary to a room once the lights go down and the clock strikes twelve on *All Hallows' Eve!*

1 Haunt Set Hack

Maximize cheap prop materials to the fullest. For example: bedsheets from a discount or thrift store. Just one set provides several yards of usable fabric. Throw them in the washer & dryer to wrinkle up. Dye them or use as is for color. Tear the ends and add a few holes. These can be hung to cover walls, draped over furniture and tables, or made into an endless variety of costume parts.

Pepper's Ghost boy captured on film is one for the guest book!

3 Haunt Set Hack

For the smaller-size skeletons think of ways to add them to furniture, like under tables or to the back of chairs. Wire the joints to pose them and use zip ties to secure them.

113

Inexpensive purchased props can be combined for a more interesting effect. Here, a raven statue is wrapped in faux barbed wire.

Use plug-in pumpkins inside. Use a multiplug outlet and group them at the base of a table or along the back of a couch.

This maid will gladly take your hat . . . and your head. The butler is ready with some finger food . . . literally.

4 Haunt Set Hack At the close of the season, when all of the home haunt sets come down and props are put away, think of better ways to pack up the holiday. Use rolling clothing racks to hang up all the skeletons together. Use another rack to attach cords from top to bottom, using multiple hooks to hang all the plastic pumpkins down the cords. Think how fun it would be to roll out the racks next year!

5 Haunt Set Hack For budget-friendly decor, temporarily stuff black plastic trash bags with any type of clothes, cloth, or more plastic bags. Use string to form human or animal shapes (*tie off head, shoulders, waist, legs, ect.*). Hang form upside down with string and spray bag with spray glue. Cover the whole surface with cheap pull-apart spider's web from a bag. Attach a few spiders to the outside. Hang the forms behind furniture, over a table, on the porch, from a tree . . . These textured bundles don't have to do anything to create the *heebie-jeebies!*

Make imaginative groupings of props. It can be funny, macabre, and scary . . . and don't forget the bugs, spiders, frogs, and snakes!

Purchase faux Spanish moss and hang it from ceilings, over mausoleums, around the buffet, or in doorways. Add layers of cheesecloth spider-webbing too!

Use wrinkled white sheets over furniture for an abandoned house look.

6 Haunt Set Hack A bar or island area is a great focal point to haunt up. Hang faux moss or ivy down from a chandelier. Group battery-operated candles around an old silver tray filled with Halloween treats. Add in a cauldron bubbler and some elegant goblets. Even the spirits would take a seat at this haunted bar!

There are many directions a haunted-house theme can take. Some are made for horror, with lots of blood, sharp instruments, and body parts. Others are more about atmosphere and suspense. And some may seem like homey yet slightly decrepit and abandoned sorts of haunted houses . . . where one might imagine ghosts wandering the dark halls at night and the echoing sounds of footsteps when no one is there. Whatever your home-haunt preference is—be sure to add the details that will convey the story your house has to tell. From the moment your visitors arrive to the moment they leave, make a statement. Plan out how your guests will move through the space and what they will see. Let your creativity spark their imagination, and your guests will leave thinking . . . *I wonder what next year will hold.*

7 Haunt Set Hack

Pile on the rats, the bats, the ravens, and skulls . . . not just one or two. Make it ten or twenty for real impact! Even if you add only a few new props to the collection every year, you are curating a special spooky vibe when you have a lot of similar items.

Every nook and cranny of the haunted house becomes a theater of the eerie and the macabre.

8 Haunt Set Hack

Believe it or not—wallpaper can be found with distressed and deteriorated wall designs. Transform even a small wall space, such as over a fireplace, by cutting foam core boards to fit wall size. Use spray glue to attach grunge wallpaper to boards and put in place over a "normal" wall. Use removable, wall-friendly, two-way tape to attach. You can also use any clearance wallpaper design and distress it yourself with paint and tearing. This is an instant way to achieve the *haunted-house* look!

It's All about the Costumes

The Mitchells take Halloween costumes very seriously. Layers of texture over layers of fabric over a store-bought or thrifted base help create the best-looking costume. Costumes are never last-minute ideas. Hours might be spent sewing on pearls or hand-cutting a thousand holes for that perfect "just out of the grave" look. Next to props, costumes are the second-most-important part of the home haunt. It's important to dress up as you go out on this most spooktacular night of the year!

1 Costume Hack Use battery-operated LED string lights as part of a costume. Lighted tiara, robot electronics, magic wand—not only will it add a fun element to the costume, but it will add a safety element to be seen at night!

3 Costume Hack Kids have so many toys they quickly outgrow. Don't get rid of them yet . . . instead see how they might be turned into costume bits. Hot-glue a bunch of faux metal parts to an old shirt with a sign that says: *Magnetic Personality*. Or attach a bunch of doll heads with messy hair with a sign that says: *Crazy Hair Day*. Or take a bag full of mismatched parts and let the kids go full cyborg, using their own imaginations!

2 Costume Hack Kids might want to have a more modern interactive costume . . . how about an oversized cardboard smartphone with an open square-space window to show their face. Hit play for a live Instagram or YouTube video. This could also be used as a photo booth idea for a Halloween party.

Mitchell Family 2015 *Halloween*

Trick or Treat

4 Costume Hack

Think great historical personas . . . *in miniature*. A child-sized Queen Victoria, Muhammad Ali, or George Washington is a fun way to connect to history and give those kids with big personalities a chance to fill some pretty big shoes for an evening. History is full of great costume ideas. Copy the main shapes, fabric colors, and props that represent that character.

5 Costume Hack

Finding ideas for this year's costume, whether for the whole family, the kids, or just yourself, can be daunting. Luckily, there are so many online resources made to help make those decisions easier. Even we have created a Pinterest mood board called *So Many Costumes*. In it we put everything from shoes, patterns, movie-based, historical, fantasy—anything that inspires or educates us throughout the year in all things costume!

The Mitchell Family

Dancing ghouls and howling lil' devils get ready to fly out into the night. There is sure to be dancing and feasting at the party. *Don't come home till the candy bag is full!*

6 Costume Hack Conjure up those past Halloweens to inspire this year's costume or decorating creations. Create a feature wall of previous years' costume photos. Kids, parents, great-great-grandparents . . . either in costume, carving the jack-o'-lanterns, or decorating the front porch.

1 **Cemetery Hack** Bring on a whole chilling flock of crows . . . not spread out all over the graveyard, but with the whole group centered on one thing or spot. One grave, one tree, one entrance arch . . . Let your guests feel outnumbered and wonder— *What strange force calls their dark eyes to gather here . . . and look at me?*

2 **Cemetery Hack**
For a touch of eerie, put two pond misters in two bowls of water and place on each side of your cemetery entrance. Tilt the bowls just enough for the mist to flow over the sides of the bowl into the path. The bowls can be under bushes or hidden behind pillars. Refill water as needed. Add a low-lying light to shine on the mist. Unlike with a fog machine, the water mist will stay on the ground.

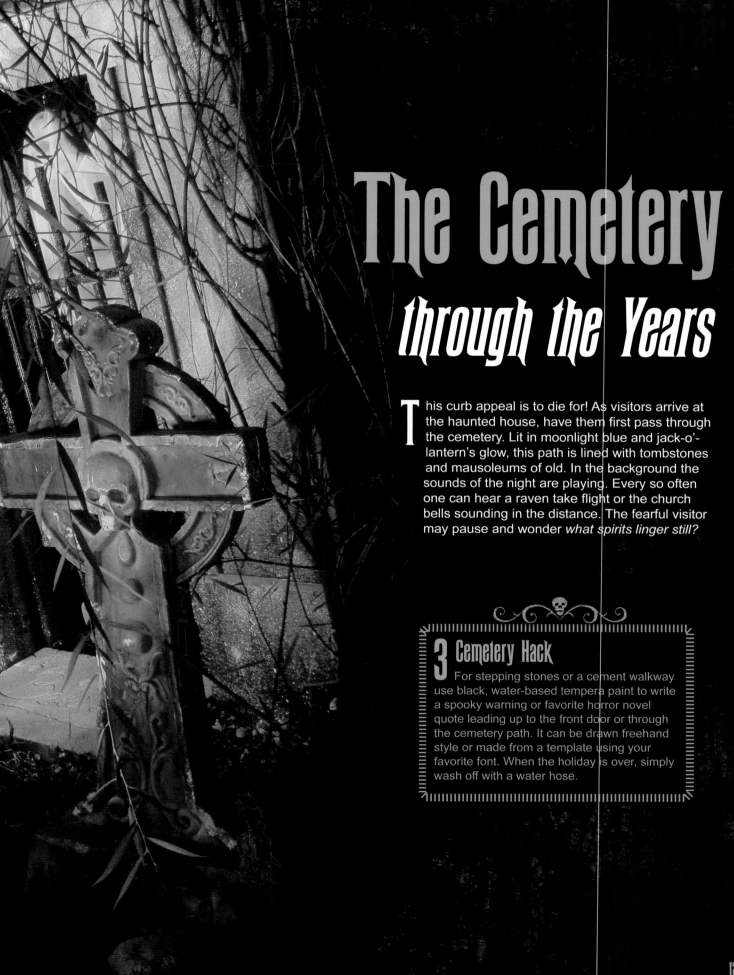

The Cemetery
through the Years

T his curb appeal is to die for! As visitors arrive at
the haunted house, have them first pass through
the cemetery. Lit in moonlight blue and jack-o'-
lantern's glow, this path is lined with tombstones
and mausoleums of old. In the background the
sounds of the night are playing. Every so often
one can hear a raven take flight or the church
bells sounding in the distance. The fearful visitor
may pause and wonder *what spirits linger still?*

3 Cemetery Hack

For stepping stones or a cement walkway
use black, water-based tempera paint to write
a spooky warning or favorite horror novel
quote leading up to the front door or through
the cemetery path. It can be drawn freehand
style or made from a template using your
favorite font. When the holiday is over, simply
wash off with a water hose.

The Mitchells are at home with everyday spirits who want to have a little fun scaring the life out of anyone brave enough to enter!

4 Cemetery Hack

If cemetery space in your yard is tight, how about creating a pint-sized pet cemetery? *Timmy the goldfish, Freddy the finch, Sam the snake.* These small pet tombstones could even fit in a planter box. Just make extra-small headstones and have fun with the small scale.

5 Cemetery Hack

Gather a collection of long, thin twigs (*free!*), dried leaves (*free!*), and faux ivy vines for an entrance, around a doorway, or draped around tombstones . . . anywhere a touch of decay and over-growth are needed. We even stuffed this scarecrow with long, dried weeds, and it just looks so much creepier than before . . . *especially when the wind rustled the branches!*

Nothing beats a scarecrow under the moonlight in the chill of an October night!

Pay no attention to the man in the window! He'll be watching your every move . . .

Add an orange light to an upstairs room and pull back the curtains. It stopped traffic at our house!

A few translucent ghosts amid the bushes to really bring the cemetery to life!

REST IN PEACE

6 Cemetery Hack

Lift a few pumpkins up off the ground. Prop them up on birdbaths, fence posts, or columns for added visual appeal.

HowTo Haunt YourHouse .com

Thank You

Through the years, *The Mitchell Cemetery* has been visited by the living, who came seeking a safe thrill and a few ghosts. Maybe they were seeking the spirit of their own Halloweens past. Or maybe they just wanted to feel like a kid again. Each year we put out our sign and invited any and all to come visit. There were more than a few laughs. A few screams. And a whole lot of fun along the way. Memories were made and new generations were inspired. We didn't set out to start a tradition at the house on Penton Street, but it evolved into one nonetheless.

From our haunted house to yours, we wish you all a special All Hallows' Eve. May your Halloween candle burn bright. May your candy cauldron stay full. And may all the spirits keep you in good company throughout the years to come!

The Mitchell Family

Credits

Font credits: Ravenscroft font was originally conceived and drawn by Tim McKenny, then refined and developed by Justin Callaghan *www.mickeyavenue.com*.

Gypsy Curse is made by Sinister Fonts and is inspired by horror movie posters of the mid-20th century.

Photography by Shawn and Lynne Mitchell. All projects in this book were made by Shawn and Lynne Mitchell for their Halloween home haunt, *The Mitchell Cemetery*.

Entering the home-haunter's world is a step into prop-building, special effects, and packed-to-the-rafters garages!

CORNELIUS VANAPTER

Even the skeletons run screaming out of the cemetery!

Shawn brought Granny to life each year!

Index